CUNARD'S THREE QUEENS

A CELEBRATION

The Royal Rendezvous: the three *Queens* – the *Queen Mary 2* far left, the *Queen Victoria* in center and the *Queen Elizabeth 2* on the right – seen at New York in January 2007. (Cunard Line).

CUNARD'S THREE QUEENS
A CELEBRATION

WILLIAM H. MILLER

AMBERLEY

To Michael Hadgis
for his cherished friendship, his great help, his wonderful support

First published 2009

Amberley Publishing Plc
Cirencester Road, Chalford,
Stroud, Gloucestershire, GL6 8PE

www.amberley-books.com

Copyright © William H. Miller 2009

The right of William H. Miller to be identified as the Author
of this work has been asserted in accordance with the
Copyrights, Designs and Patents Act 1988.

ISBN 978 1 84868 364 8

British Library Cataloguing in Publication Data.
A catalogue record for this book is available from the
British Library.

Typeset in 10pt on 12pt Sabon.
Typesetting and Origination by FONTHILLDESIGN.
Printed in the UK.

CONTENTS

Foreword   7

Acknowledgments   8

2008: The Year of Three Queens   9

    January   9

    April & May   33

October 2008: Farewell voyages on the *QE2*   63

Bibliography   120

FOREWORD

On a Tuesday evening in March 2009, I was among the invited guests summoned to the Grand Hyatt Hotel in midtown Manhattan. The occasion was quite special: Carol Marlow, the president of the great Cunard Line, was 'unveiling' plans for the new *Queen Elizabeth*. It was some eighteen months before the new 90,000-ton ship would be commissioned. The reception included a preview of the ship's grand, Art Deco-style interiors as well as formal announcement of her first six voyages, including her maiden voyage, a two-week Southampton-Atlantic Isles cruise. A third *Queen* was coming and it was all very exciting!

Previously, 2008 had been a very significant, very historic year – for the first time, there were three Cunard *Queens* in service. Myself, I was aboard the *QE2*'s crossing from New York to Southampton that April. She was, of course, a very special ship to me. I made many voyages on her, including the 30th-anniversary cruise in June 1999 with no fewer than 600 ship enthusiasts onboard. That was perhaps the greatest group of its kind ever to put to sea. The late Frank Braynard, John Maxtone-Graham and our author, my good friend Bill Miller, were aboard as guest speakers. Other notables included Richard Faber, Hisashi Noma (Japan's foremost maritime historian) and, for lunch, the late Commodore Leroy Alexanderson (the last master of the *United States*). I have always liked the *QE2* very much and it all seemed right and proper to pay full homage to her.

By 2004, I had my first trips aboard the *Queen Mary 2*, another wonderful liner. Like many, I was delighted, even thrilled, that Cunard – and all thanks to Carnival and their great investment – would continue and prosper, and that traditional Atlantic crossings were part of the company's bright future. The towering *QM2* was a fine successor not only to the *QE2*, but to the original *Queen Mary* and *Queen Elizabeth*. But in January 2008, I traveled on the brand-new *Queen Victoria* and fell madly in love with her. Quickly, she became a great favorite.

In 2009, I traveled again on both the *Queen Mary 2* and the *Queen Victoria*. Both liners offer wonderful shipboard experiences – fine food, excellent service, wonderful entertainment. I treasure my days aboard them and that Cunard remains the very great company that it has been for some 170 years. And now, to record another chapter in Cunard history, covering the year of the three *Queens*, I am thrilled to see another of Bill's books, this one documenting a trio of royal maritime ladies. Hail to the *Queen Elizabeth 2*, the *Queen Mary 2* and the *Queen Victoria*!

Thomas Cassidy
Editor, *Ocean & Cruise News*
Northport, New York
April 2009

ACKNOWLEDGEMENTS

Preparing any book, but especially one on the iconic Cunard *Queens* is a group effort. I am the 'cruise director' of sorts of a varied team of otherwise superb, very generous and often most patient helping hands. Enormous thanks to the great Cunard Line itself – to Jackie Chase, John Duffy, Eric Flounders, Michael Gallagher, Caroline Mathieson, Carol Marlow, Brian O'Connor and Julia Young at the Cunard offices on both sides of the Atlantic – and to the wonderful, ever-kind and supportive staff and crew aboard the great Cunard liners. Very special thanks also to Bea Muller, Robert Welding and John Whitworth. And, of course, very special thanks to Campbell McCutcheon, editor, publisher and keenest of liner enthusiasts himself, and to Amberley Publishing Company for taking on this project.

Further appreciation to a team of 'first-class' assistants: the late Frank Braynard, Tom Cassidy, Richard Faber, Michael Hadgis and Abe Michaelson. And, no less, to a splendid 'crew' that also appreciate the great Cunard *Queens*: Dr Nelson Arnstein, Philippe Brebant, J.K. Byass, Stephen Card, Jim Carlisle, Tom Chirby, Anthony Cooke, Luis Miguel Correia, Charles Cotton, Maurizio Eliseo, Rose Everett, Stanley Haviland, Brian Hawley, Andy Hernandez, John Heywood, Pine Hodges, Charles Howland, Peter Knego, Des Kirkpatrick, Arnold Kludas, Alec and Mhairi Laing, Robert Lloyd, Shirley Matchett, John Maxtone-Graham, Hisashi Noma, Robert O'Brien, Mark Perry, Mario Pulice, David Rulon, Der Scutt, Jeffrey Towns, Ann and Etta Uttley, Douglas Ward, Commodore Ronald and Mrs Kim Warwick, Albert Wilhelmi, Captain Robin Woodall and Ian and Lauren Wright.

Companies, organizations and other entities that deserve a nod of appreciation include the Cunard Line, Port of Port Everglades Authority, South Street Seaport Museum, Steamship Historical Society of America, the World Ocean & Cruise Liner Society and the World Ship Society.

2008: THE YEAR OF THREE QUEENS

January 2008: The Three *Queens* in New York

No ships attract more attention than the Cunard *Queens*. The *Queen Mary 2*'s naming by Queen Elizabeth II and her maiden voyage in January 2004 were huge publicity events. The same ship's maiden arrival into New York that April deeply aroused and excited all television and radio stations as well as the newspapers. (In fact, I was up and out by 3:00am to do three TV news programs, to highlight the *Mary*'s maiden arrival in the Big Apple.) Even the normally less-than-interested-in-ships *New York Times* ran a front-page feature as well as a large photo of the huge *QM2*. Soon after, the *QM2* and her older fleetmate, the *Queen Elizabeth 2*, ran a six-day tandem crossing from New York to Southampton. That too was big news.

In February 2006, I was happily aboard the 17-deck-high *QM2* as she made her first visits to San Francisco and then to Sydney. At the Australian port, she had yet another double-crown rendezvous with the beloved *Elizabeth 2*. Both were huge publicity events, highly successful for the ever-busy teams of Cunard publicists. Some 3 million spectators, both ashore and afloat, came out at Sydney to see the two Cunard *Queens*. Whistles honked, cameras flashed and fireworks filled the summer evening skies. 'The event was pure magic. The harbor was crammed with small boats – including dozens of seemingly top-heavy charter spectator vessels. And the two *Queens* played their parts as well and, in well-lighted splendor, both looked absolutely regal, truly royal,' said Des Kirkpatrick, a New Yorker who had come down on the *QM2*.

In 2008, at New York in January and then in April at Southampton, Cunard seemed to pull out all stops. For the very first time ever, three *Queens* were together – the *QM2*, *QE2* and the new *Queen Victoria*. Indeed, it was an eye-opening collection of Cunard superliners. In all, it was some 320,000 combined tons of ocean liner spectacle. Excitement was high, hearts were warmed and even a few tears flowed. Deep sentiment, in fact budding and bubbling nostalgia, was already being cast toward the 39-year-old *Elizabeth 2*, which was leaving Cunard service and scheduled in November for a new life as moored hotel, museum and entertainment center out in Dubai. Probably the most beloved ship afloat, the *QE2* will leave behind a wonderful legacy – she has snatched just about every record (most miles steamed, more passengers carried, more world ports visited, etc.) for a superliner. She has been immensely successful, hugely popular and the longest-serving Cunarder of all time. Legions of loyalists love her – her six farewell voyages and cruises that began in September sold out completely in seven hours!

But the three *Queens* at New York on a January's night had some prior worries – the *Queen Victoria* was running late as she crossed from Southampton and then, complicating things and adding to the worries, a nasty mix of rain and snow were predicted for that evening. Happily, the *Victoria* made it on time and only a chilly rain intruded slightly as the three super ships gathered in the Upper Bay off the Statue of Liberty for fireworks, salutes and more horn honking. It all took less than an hour, but what an amazing sight! The three liners were aglow like jeweled boxes laying on glass and all against the ever-magical, well-lighted Manhattan skyline. Spectator and dinner boats were booked solid months in advance. 'I would not have missed it for the world,' said a liner enthusiast, who made a 10-hour drive from Ohio.

Sunday, 13 January

'The Cunard lion is roaring again!' So said Cunard President and Managing Director Carol Marlow during today's maiden voyage reception for the new *Queen Victoria*. Hours later, on the clearest of winter nights, the 90,000-tonner departed and ocean liner history was made. In highly choreographed order and for the first time in maritime annals, three Cunard *Queens* – the month-old *Victoria,* the bigger *Queen Mary 2* and the veteran, but much-beloved *Queen Elizabeth 2* – departed together and then met, in something of a royal review, off the Statue of Liberty. With the glittering Manhattan skyline against a charcoal sky as a backdrop, the Cunarder was sparkling, glowing, like bejeweled boxes. Music filled the air, little boats and charter craft were top heavy with spectators and all while colorful fireworks lighted the wintry sky for the grand salute. I was aboard the *Victoria,* starting her fourth voyage and beginning her first cruise around the world. Expectedly, the new Cunarder was booked to capacity, 2,000 in all and with as many as 700 making the full 105-night circumnavigation. It was all a grand beginning to a special voyage aboard what some guests had already dubbed as their favorite *Queen.*

Cunard is perhaps the best-known name in ocean liner history. The 168-year-old company is today being revived, almost re-invented, certainly rejuvenated. Ten years ago, in 1998, however, Cunard was fading. Their fleet consisted of the 29-year-old, 70,000-ton *Queen Elizabeth 2* and the 25-year-old, 24,000-ton *Vistafjord.* But then Miami-based Carnival Corporation moved in and saved the day, buying the historic firm for $600 million and then investing a further $800 million to build the 151,000-ton, 2,600-passenger *Queen Mary 2,* completed in late 2003 and then the largest liner yet built. While used as a cruise ship at times, her main purpose was to carry on a grand, often cherished Cunard tradition: North Atlantic crossings between New York and Southampton. And now further expansion has followed: the $600 million, 90,000-ton *Queen Victoria* joined the fleet last December and, costing another $600 million-plus, the 92,000-ton *Queen Elizabeth* is due out in the fall of 2010. The 70,000-ton *Queen Elizabeth 2* left the Cunard roster in November, having been sold to Dubai interests for $100 million and for further use, but as a moored hotel, museum and entertainment center, and now as a floating hotel in Capetown, South Africa, for the 2010 Soccer World Cup.

Looking back, Cunard's first ship, the 1,100-ton *Britannia,* crossed the Atlantic from Liverpool to Boston in fourteen days, in the summer of 1840. At best, this paddle and sail vessel with its single orange-red and black funnel could make a mere 9 knots and carried a maximum of 115 passengers. Comparatively, the 207ft-long *Britannia* could easily fit inside the Britannia Restaurant of the current 1,132ft-long *Queen Mary 2.* Success followed, however, and the company's ships grew larger and faster and emphasized safety. Within sixty-five years, by 1907, the 32,000-ton *Lusitania* and *Mauretania* were not only the largest and most opulent liners afloat, but also the world's fastest. Their Liverpool-New York crossings took six days. They carried some 2,165 passengers in three classes: 563 in palatial, upper-deck first class, 464 in somewhat less luxurious second class and then 1,138 in lower-deck third class, the infamous steerage. Even larger, the stunning *Aquitania* followed in 1914. In the 1920s and with a fleet of over two-dozen liners, Cunard's all-important express service, now based at Southampton, was run by three of the world's greatest and grandest ocean liners – the *Mauretania, Aquitania* and, largest of all, the 52,000-ton *Berengaria.* But even better and bigger days were ahead. The 81,000-ton *Queen Mary* was commissioned in 1936 and made record runs across the North Atlantic of 3½ days. She was the fastest ship afloat. Her running-mate, the slightly larger, 83,000-ton *Queen Elizabeth,* was completed in 1940. They became heroic Second World War troop transports, the pride of the British fleet and the most successful and popular pair of superliners of their time.

The *Queen Mary* lived on to make 1,000 crossings between New York and Southampton. In the 1950s, Cunard had twelve liners in Atlantic service and their operations were perhaps best described by the company's very apt motto: 'Getting there was half the fun!' Lower-deck tourist-class fares were priced from $150 in 1955 for the five-night passages between New York and Southampton. An upper-deck suite went for $1,200. Fortunate dogs went in top-deck kennels for $25.

Above left: Rising steel formation: the iconic *QE2* under construction in 1966. (Der Scutt Collection).

Above right: The shipping world awaits: the *QE2* fitting out on the Clyde in 1968. (J.K. Byass Collection).

Right: Said to be the last of the superliners, the *QE2* passes the *France* off Norfolk, Virginia, in a view dated March 1973. (Cunard Line).

Above left: The height of 1960s modernity: the innovative Queens Room aboard the *QE2*. (Cunard Line).

Above right: Young Pine and his mother aboard the *QE2* during the ship's visit to New York in July 1969. (Pine Hodges Collection).

Left: Young ship enthusiast Pine Hodges (second on the left) views the brand-new *QE2* in a scene at New York dated July 1969. (Pine Hodges Collection).

Above: The new age of superliners: the *Queen Mary 2* under construction at St-Nazaire, France, in 2003. (Maurizio Eliseo Collection).

Right: Cosmetic touches for royalty – the *Queen Mary 2* receives her first hull painting in the summer of 2003. (Maurizio Eliseo Collection).

These pages: A fine collection of views of the mighty *Queen Mary* 2 as the 151,000-ton ship goes off on her speed trials in September 2003. (Cunard Line).

Maiden arrival at Southampton, December 2003. (Cunard Line).

Above left: Three months after entering service, the *Queen Mary 2* arrives at New York for the first time on 22 April 2004. (John McFarland Collection).

Above right: As seen from the Battery Seawall in Lower Manhattan, a fireboat sprays red, white and blue water as a part of the gala welcome. (John McFarland Collection).

Right: As the *Queen* approaches her berth along New York City's 'Luxury Liner Row', the cruise ship *Maxim Gorky* can be seen to the right. (John McFarland Collection).

Above left: The tallest liner ever to call at New York, the *Queen* approaches her berth at the foot of West 52nd Street in Manhattan. (Charles Cotton Collection).

Above right: Moran tugs assist the *Queen* as she berths at Pier 92. (John McFarland Collection).

Left: The classic royal rendezvous: the *Queen Mary 2* meets her grand predecessor, the *Queen Mary* of 1936, during a special occasion at Long Beach, California in February 2006. (Cunard Line).

Above left: Maritime majesty: the view from the *Queen Mary*'s port-side bridge wing. (Charles Cotton Collection).

Above right: The last of the three-stackers. (Author's Collection).

Right: Floodlit by night: the *Queen Mary* creates a magical effect. (Peter Knego Collection).

Below: Ticket to the launch of the *Queen Mary*. (J&C McCutcheon Collection).

Above left: In the heyday of the Atlantic liners, this view dated 1950 along New York's 'Luxury Liner Row' has three Cunarders at berth: the *Mauretania* is on the left, the *Queen Mary* in the center and the *Britannic* on the right. (John McFarland Collection).

Above right: The *Mauretania* departs in this view from April 1959 and with six other passenger liners in the background (from left to right): the *Media*, *Queen Mary* and the *Ivernia* of Cunard, the *Liberté* of the French Line, the *United States* of the United States Lines and then the Italian Line's *Giulio Cesare*. (James McNamara Collection).

Left: The largest liner in the world for decades, the 83,673-ton *Queen Elizabeth* is aglow at Pier 90, New York. (Cronican-Arroyo Collection).

Opposite: A summer's morning, dated 5 July 1961, with no less than seven liners together: (from left to right) the *Independence*, *America*, *United States*, *Olympia*, the aircraft carrier USS *Intrepid*, the *Queen Elizabeth* just docking, *Mauretania* and the *Sylvania*. (John McFarland Collection).

Above: The *Queen Elizabeth* at berth at New York in 1964, with the Italian liner *Cristoforo Colombo* just arriving. (Albert Wilhelmi Collection).

Left: The *Queen Elizabeth 2* at sea as seen from the *Queen Mary 2*. (John McFarland Collection).

Above left: During her 1994 world cruise, the *QE2* is seen berthed at Sydney's Circular Quay. (Author's Collection).

Above right: Cunard trio: the *QE2* at Port Everglades, Florida in 1994 with the *Sagafjord* on the left and the *Vistafjord* on the right. (Port of Port Everglades Authority).

Right: Getting away at Lisbon. (Luis Miguel Correia Collection).

Left: The *QE2* is to the right in this view in Norway's majestic Geirangerfjord – and with the Italian cruise ship *Valtur Prima* on the left. (Cunard Line).

Right: The great bow section facing New York City's West Side. (John McFarland Collection).

Above left: New propellers, during her re-engining refit at Bremerhaven. (J&C McCutcheon collection).

Above right: On her first outward sailing following her re-engining and installation of her 'new' funnel, the *QE2* passes the World Trade Center in this view dated May 1987. (John McFarland Collection).

Right: Painting her port of registry at Bremerhaven. (J&C McCutcheon Collection).

Above left: Christmas Eve 1996: the *QE2* at St Thomas. (Peter Knego Collection).

Above right: Berthed at Port Everglades, Florida. (Port of Port Everglades Authority).

Left: Arriving at New York. (Charles Cotton Collection).

Above left: Departing from Lisbon on 26 October 2006. (Luis Miguel Correia Collection).

Above right: Her Majesty Queen Elizabeth II is welcomed aboard the *QE2* during Cunard's 150th-anniversary celebrations in July 1990. (Cunard Line).

Right: The author (center) with friends and family aboard the *QE2* in May 1996. (Author's Collection).

Left: At Bermuda in May 1996. (John McFarland Collection).

Opposite page: The *QE2* in her short-lived grey livery. (J&C McCutcheon collection).

Right: Spectacular: another view in the Geirangerfjord. (John McFarland Collection).

Above left: In Norwegian waters, in July 1995. (John McFarland Collection).

Above right: Another view of three Cunard liners: the *Sagafjord* is in the foreground in this 1994 photo while the *QE2* and the *Vistafjord* are berthed just behind. (Port of Port Everglades Authority).

Left: Outbound at New York in 2006. (John McFarland Collection).

Above: The two *Queens* met for the first time at New York in April 2004. (Cunard Line).

Right: Preparing for a glorious tandem crossing of the Atlantic, the *Queen Mary 2* departs first. (Cunard Line).

Below: The Manhattan skyline frames the *Queen Mary 2* as she departs. (Cunard Line).

HOTEL MANAGER JOHN DUFFY

Some passengers actually cried as they disembarked from the legendary *QE2* last April, having just completed a six-night crossing from New York. When the 70,000-ton liner reached Southampton, she had also completed her final 105-day-long winter cruise (this year around South America and then around the Pacific). Some passengers that disembarked had traveled on the ship on countless voyages – some for years, sometimes for decades. She's iconic with a huge, very loyal following. 'I've booked the final voyage in November and it will cost $7,000 [on a passenger ticket], but it will be worth it,' said a senior Cunard officer, assigned to the *Queen Mary 2*. 'The *QE2* was my first ship and a great part of my life. I want to see her end, her last days with Cunard!'

The 963ft-long *QE2* is the most famous ocean liner afloat and the most successful superliner of all time, even more so in ways than the original *Queen Mary* and *Queen Elizabeth*. 'She has great fame, the most famous and most successful ocean liner of all time,' said John Duffy, the ship's Hotel Manager since 1981. We crossed together yet again just last April, on an eastbound passage from New York to Southampton. She was booked to capacity, in fact a dozen or so would-be passengers had to be turned away, apologetically sent to posh Manhattan hotels and promised a future voyage. But legions were aware that time was running out – the 39-year-old *QE2* then had but a few more months of cruising. She had, in fact, only two further visits to New York. 'There are lots of very sad people and their withdrawal has already begun,' added Duffy in the confines of his onboard office. 'When we arrive at Southampton on 18 April, many passengers will leave for the last time. There will be tears, even days before. There has been

a surge in bookings for the final season, of course, and I am told that the very last trip to Dubai sold out in 36 minutes. That's a record in itself!

'The summer and early fall cruises are also all but booked up solid,' he added. 'She has been selling like crazy. The farewell has been the spark. We even have some staff members such as maître d' David Chambers, who has been aboard since 1969. At the very end, I am sure that there will be a huge, but tearful send-off at Southampton. In reality, of course, nothing is forever – the day had to come! Personally, I am very pleased that she has found a good home, to be properly preserved and used as a functioning hotel and museum. She has been sold in her complete state. Everything goes with her to Dubai including all the Cunard memorabilia. Of course, in mega-rich Dubai, she will be looked after in old age and she will be a great tourist attraction, even as a venue for shore excursions on Cunard world cruises.'

In the meantime, the 28-knot *QE2*, still the fastest liner afloat (capable of as much as 32½ knots if needed), has several months of happy, if sentimental cruising ahead. She even had a rejuvenating, nine-day refit in mid-April while lying in the Southampton Docks. In grand tribute, Her Majesty Queen Elizabeth II is visiting in early June and some special cruises such as the 'Farewell to the British Isles' cruise are scheduled in late September. And then there is the meeting of the three *Queens* at Southampton on 22 April. On the last crossings to and from New York, the *QE2* will sail in tandem with the *QM2*. 'It is a new generation – time to pass on,' concluded John Duffy. 'Ships, like time, move on – and requirements change. The *QM2* is exquisite, the grand successor, and the new *Queen Victoria* takes over the *QE2*'s UK-based cruising role. All in all, it is a wonderful evolution!'

Left: The *Queen Victoria* and the *QE2*, Fort Lauderdale. (Cunard).

April 2008: Eastbound on the *Queen Elizabeth 2*

Robert O'Brien had not crossed the North Atlantic by liner and so it seemed fitting that he was aboard the legendary *QE2* and no less than onboard one of her very last eastbound crossings from New York to Southampton. The liner had returned to Manhattan, using the city's West Side piers, the once very popular 'Luxury Liner Row', following her 95-day-long winter cruise around South America and the Pacific. The ship was in fact overbooked and more than a dozen passengers could not be accommodated at the last minute. Disappointed, they were sent to New York City hotels, with promises of hefty compensation on future voyages. On 12 April 2008, the legendary *QE2* set sail on a six-day transatlantic crossing to her home port of Southampton. O'Brien, a fledgling ocean liner historian and collector, was captivated by the opportunity to sail the great *Elizabeth* and in the final months of her long, distinguished Cunard career. He later wrote, 'While not her last crossing, it was quite memorable for many reasons. It all began as we backed out of the berth in NY as a number of helicopters, and a few salutes from small craft would be a prelude to what this great liner would receive in six months. On the second day at sea the *QE2* came to a slow crawl over the very same position where the *Titanic* had foundered exactly 96 years before. A rare occasion, and almost everyone onboard gathered at the fantail to see the laying of the wreath and a long pause to remember those that were lost on that fateful day. There were lectures almost every day and of various types with a special one given by Commodore Ronald Warwick about his rare opportunity to dive on the world's most famous wreck [the *Titanic*]. A passing sea with fair skies, *QE2* trivia, photo opportunities, as well as boat-loads of souvenirs and new shipmates followed as we steamed eastward where gloomy weather awaited us at Southampton.'

Saturday, 12 April

The *QE2* glistened in the late-afternoon, springtime sunshine. She had, in ways, and especially after more than 700 visits, almost become a part of the New York cityscape. She was berthed at Pier 92, at West 52nd Street. Before departure, the Steamship Historical Society's Long Island, New York chapter organized a visit, tour and drinks party (held in the Yacht Club onboard) of the great Cunarder. Many had sailed her in the past. Expectedly, it was a sell-out and, so thoughtfully, was also made into a 'launching party' for my latest book, *The QE2: A Picture History*. An exciting afternoon, I signed some 120 copies in little more than an hour and somehow managed a chat for almost everyone. Of course, many

are friends and others are ship enthusiast acquaintances. Adding to the celebration, retired Commodore Ron Warwick made a guest appearance (he was sailing as well) and offered to co-sign some of the books. Indeed, no ship afloat had the cache of the *QE2* and she was soon ending her Cunard career. It was ocean liner history.

Soon after tea at 4 o'clock in the grand Queens Room (and where there wasn't a seat to be had from 3 o'clock onwards), many made their way to the outer decks for the posted 5:00pm sailing. But planning went astray, as the fueling from a barge was not yet complete. Even Queens have to wait. 6 o'clock turned to 7 o'clock and it was closer to 8 before we cast off. By then, the famed Manhattan skyline was cast in an orange-turning-to-cinnamon-colored glow. The lights of the great towers were being switched on. The *Queen* made her exit. Moran tugs gently guided her into the mid-Hudson and then off we went, sailing south along the river, into the Lower Bay and finally under the imposing Verrazano-Narrows Bridge and out to sea in the charcoal night. I did the harbor narrative from the port bridge wing, pointing out the highlights and also adding a detail here and there. As the leading lady on a great stage, the *Queen* was amidst the most glorious set: the twinkling skyscrapers, lighted craft buzzing about the harbor, great highpoints such as the floodlit Statue of Liberty. It was, in ways, the beginning of a sentimental journey.

Monday, 21 April

Mist on the moors! I could see my breath as we prayed and sang in Fodsley Church, a tiny charm of a 400-year-old, stone place tucked away in the quiet English countryside, in very rural Shropshire. A fog bank drizzled over the nearby valley, a classic manor house or two were thoughtfully (and considerately) poised on the hillside. The mood was of total serenity – not a soul in sight as we later tooled through the backroads and tightly crammed lanes in the stately blue Jag. Afterward, a grand luncheon in a stately, pillared Georgian mansion, sitting at an endlessly long, highly polished mahogany table with Lord and Lady Mansfield, friends of Howard Franklin, a friend of mine for some 30 years. Both of them are deliciously charming, 50-something-year-olds with, well of course, a yacht, another grand house but out in sunny Spain and, rather expectedly, buckets of money. He's a publishing tycoon; she's richer still (from a long, very distinguished family). Their garden, seen through great double doors, seemed to stretch for miles while the innards of their very grand home are pure, charming 'English country' from end to end: the thickly gilt-framed paintings, the gleaming, mirror-like period furniture, a dozen or so of those overstuffed, well-pillowed sofas. There were a dozen or so cars in the household garages – including a 1934 Rolls that Jean Harlow might have used.

Lunch took hours, the classic English Sunday courses, the perfectly cooked roast beef, an array of specially selected wines. I was in glorious company, seated next to the private secretary of Princess Anne and, to the other side, to one of London's finest interior decorators, herself a lady of stunning, anecdote-filled background. ('I tend to wear Mother's tiara only once or twice a year these days,' she grinningly told me.) There were two dozen guests in all and – thoughtfully – a toast in fluted Waterford to my upcoming 60th. Last week, having crossed on the QE2 from New York, the ship was overflowing to the very last upper bunk as she is soon off, bringing tears to some eyes, to a new life in Dubai (as a moored hotel and museum) beginning in November. Loyalty to her is extraordinary. Some passengers wept openly as they disembarked at Southampton last Friday – it was, after all, their last time aboard that cherished 39-year-old ocean-going legend.

I trained northward to Shropshire, to Howard's place, his noble, wonderfully comfortable house that is a charming haven of another age, gracious living, the highest cozy comforts. Of course, there has been, amidst a cup of tea here and a G&T there, a virtual non-stop schedule – luncheons, dinners, a museum visit or two, an art exhibition, a Saturday night house party for, well, sixty, but who was really counting. But the great moods – those fog-shrouded nights, the chilly, almost icy mornings, that poetic English countryside silence (PBS drama, indeed) punctuated only with the sounds of chirping birds and the odd bark of, say, some black Labrador. April has been especially chilly and damp up in these parts – gloves and scarves are well needed.

Tuesday, 22 April

Made the 10:20 down from Church Stretton, near Howard, and with a change at Newport (in Wales), connected on to Southampton. I was boarding the Queen Mary 2 by 3pm. En route, bright sunshine adds to the mood as we wind our way throughout the countryside, stop at small villages and sidings, and then into the larger stations in places such as steeple-lined Bath. A new, superbly maintained train, it still had the lolling rattle as it passed over tracks, which altogether adds to a charmingly relaxing ride on the rails. We made Southampton Central by 2 and, while the city seemed to be buzzing with lots of outbound passengers heading for the port area, the run over to the Queen Elizabeth II Terminal and the Queen Mary 2 was all made with incredible ease. The taxi driver

remarked, 'With the three Queens in port, it reminds me of the old days, the way Southampton used to be when those great Atlantic liners were sailing. I remember days when we would have five or six liners sailing in one day – from Cunard, Holland America, P&O, Union Castle and Royal Mail Lines. It was a wonderful era that passed all to quickly, or so it seems, and is missed by many, many people. Myself, I will be watching later as the Queens depart. It is a once-in-a-lifetime occasion!'

It was a special day for anyone even remotely interested in ships, the great liners, Cunard, the infamous Queens. As in New York in January, the three Queens were together at Southampton. The Mary was sailing that evening for New York, the Victoria was heading off on a cruise to the Med and all while the QE2 was alongside undergoing a small refit and some repairs (and being made ready for her handing over to her new owners in Dubai in seven months). The April event was blessed with warm, spring sunshine at Southampton. The three ships were radiant. With blasts on her throaty whistle and as the smallish Pacific Princess almost quietly slipped past, the QM2 departed from the Queen Elizabeth II Terminal. Instead of heading out, however, she went in the opposite direction and, at a slow, well-regulated harbor speed, she proceeded to a planned spot off the Western Docks and just opposite to the old King George V Graving Dock, a 1934-built repair facility that in fact had just been closed. The 1,132ft-long Mary then paused, turned and, with seemingly great ease, reversed course, passing Elizabeth 2, which was undergoing a dockside refit at Berth 106 in those Western Docks, but with her Cunard crew lining the outer, upper decks. The whistles of both Queens sounded – almost endlessly – and as passengers waved tiny plastic Union Jack flags, heard mood-stirring songs such as 'Rule Britannia' and 'Land of Hope & Glory' played out over the Mary's public address system and, somehow interwoven, I managed something of an ocean-liner-history-filled narrative, broadcast from the QM2's towering bridge.

The mighty, seventeen-deck Mary moved slowly, majestically, regally making her way past the ever-handsome-looking Elizabeth 2 and then passing the four-month-old Queen Victoria, which was further along, at Berth 101, and already loaded with 2,000 passengers bound for a Mediterranean cruise. Those whistles continued their back-and-forth salutes; small craft loyally floated in their 'royal escort' along the outer, starboard side and then, in a slight April evening haze, the Mary signaled with a final triple blast on her whistles (one of them coming, in fact, from the original, 1936-built Queen Mary at Los Angeles) and headed into the Solent. With a turn to the right at the Isle of Wight, she was off to the Atlantic and another six-night crossing to New York. Dutifully, the Queen

Victoria followed, being sort of the royal princess following the queen. The *QE2*, the queen mother, remained at the pier, gradually and poetically disappearing in the mist-filled, light-sapphire-colored twilight.

'No company can create special events with its ships like Cunard,' said a loyal and faithful passenger from Manhattan. 'The *Queens* are so incredibly famous and, of course, Cunard has such a rich and colorful history. Like all the "king's horses", there was the original *Queen Mary* and *Queen Elizabeth*, then the *Queen Elizabeth 2*, now the *Queen Mary 2* and *Queen Victoria* and, on the great horizon, the new *Queen Elizabeth* in 2010. What a wonderful collection of great and grand ships!'

Sunday, 27 April

It is the final day, moody and gray, of the six-night westbound passage from Southampton to New York. Having come over on the *QE2* and now returning on the *QM2*, it was almost back to the golden age of Cunard, using two great liners (just like the original *Mary* and *Elizabeth*) and when 'getting there was half the fun!'

It has been a glorious westward passage – the ship stunning and splendidly served and fed, the staff very friendly and often quite impeccable, but the fellow guests a highlight. Met so many interesting fellow voyagers – among the 1,200 British travelers, there were 400 from the *Queen Victoria*'s world cruise and a sprinkling of other Europeans. One classically beautiful British woman jumps to mind, however. Now living in America, she told me that she 'emigrated' to the States some 41 years ago, on the last crossing to New York of the *Queen Mary*. 'It was quite an experience,' she said, gently grabbing her triple strand of aged pearls. 'I was moving to Connecticut and so sailed with three children, six dogs and seventy-nine pieces of luggage!'

Of course, the lectures prompt fellow passengers to come forth. 'I was a captain with the old Brocklebank Line. We ran freighters out to India and the Middle East,' said an elderly man supported by a hand-carved wooden cane. A lady in a bright red hat comes forth, 'Just wanted to tell you that I was born in South Africa and first came to England in 1949. We sailed, of course. The ship was still in wartime mode, all very basic and with lots of dormitories and the most awful food and practically no service. It was called the *Carnarvon Castle*.' Another lady, this one from Cornwall, tells me that she was named Amra. It seems that her father was an officer with the British India Line and, amongst the ships on which he'd served, the passenger liner *Amra* was one of them. He was, in fact, sailing from Bombay aboard the *Amra* on the very day that she was born back home in England.

Another lady, a former New York City high school teacher, all but whispers to me that she often went to Europe in the 1950s and '60s, but always by freighter. 'I liked the calm, quiet, very relaxing atmosphere of a dozen or even less passengers,' she said. 'I remember the *American Shipper* taking me to London and then another trip, but on an Italian freighter that sailed from Genoa to Baltimore. Another time, I came home from Copenhagen, on a Danish ship with only three other passengers. My first liner did not come for years, until the late '90s, when I finally decided to cross on the *QE2*.'

Michael (my cabin mate this trip) has been keenly observant, his increasingly astute nautical eye reviewing these grand ladies of maritime lore. (He was aboard his very first cruise, on Holland America's *Veendam*, just last October and then had traveled with me onboard the *Queen Victoria* last January and aboard the *Queen Elizabeth 2* just last week. In quick time, he has now sailed all three of Cunard's *Queens*.) And so the white smoke went up this morning – his final, detailed scores are in. According to 'First Mate Mike', the *Queen Victoria* has the slight edge. She wins in his final tallies, having a few added points based on our 17-night jaunt aboard that brand-new liner last January. The *Mary* follows as his close second, of course, and all while the dear, classic *Elizabeth 2* scores third. He actually liked the *QE2* very much, but the *Victoria* and the *Mary* are 'wow ships' of today.

And so, those goodbye and parting words fill out this day … 'We'll keep in touch' … 'I have your card' … 'See you on another voyage' … and 'I'll send you that menu from my mother's trip on the *Queen Elizabeth* in 1949'.

New York harbor appears off the bow tomorrow at 6:00am.

Monday, 28 April

Springtime in New York: floods of rain, fog and no visibility. We are at Cunard's terminal in Red Hook, Brooklyn, firmly secured alongside and not even the faint silhouette of the famed Lower Manhattan skyline. And, of course, no sight of the Statue of Liberty either. Disappointing, of course, and especially for those on their first arrival by ship at New York. But we are all ashore quite quickly and effortlessly.

No longer caressed by the strong arms of 'Mother Cunard', the passengers wait along curbsides, often with worried eyes, for family and friends, for taxis and hired cars, and for bus connections to airports and those flights home.

Thursday, 1 May

An otherwise very empty flight (on Jet Blue) takes me out to California, directly to Long Beach, and where I am soon settled aboard the *Queen*

Mary and in the very roomy Duke & Duchess of Windsor Suite. It is a weekend of events: seeing friends and fellow collectors, participating and also speaking at a convention themed to the SS *United States* (and the long struggle to at least save her from the scrapheap) and, on Saturday, to celebrate my 60th birthday.

Friday, 2 May
An exhibition about another great liner, the brilliant SS *United States*, was formally opened with speeches, recollections of that maritime speed champion and a celebratory cocktail party.

Saturday, 3 May
The legendary *Queen Mary* set the stage for a weekend of ocean liner festivities, celebrations and even inaugurals. 'What a great place to have these events, onboard the fantastic *Queen Mary*, the last of the great ocean liners of the golden age, from the 1930s,' said an attendee from Seattle.

During the day, there were lunches, get-togethers and of course lectures and talks – on such topics as the Blue Riband, the history of the 1959-built *Rotterdam* and general ocean liner lore. Myself, I gave an afternoon talk – in the *Mary*'s stunning Deco-rich Main Lounge – on the life and times of the *United States* and other American passenger ships dating from the 1950s and '60s. A highlight, however, was the standing-room-only premier of the brilliant new documentary 'Lady in Waiting: The Story of the SS *United States*'. A 60-minute *tour de force* of superb visuals, sights, sounds and on-camera interviews (including myself), it has been expertly created by producers Mark Perry (currently with television's *Ghost Whisperer*)

and Robert Radler, and has been sold for subsequent television viewing to no less than 80 PBS stations across America. (The New York City showing will be, for example, on 4 July.) Aptly, the film received a loud standing ovation as a conclusion. Then there was a black-tie dinner, staged in the equally Deco-style Cabin Class Dining Room, and which included a very kind and thoughtful birthday celebration for me, highlighted by a cake made to resemble a funnel from the *United States* and with a notation on the top: 'Still Smoking at 60'!

Sunday, 4 May
As a few began to disperse, some of us continued our friendly gatherings with visits to the homes of some world-class ocean liner collectors. 'It was one of the very best ocean liner occasions I've ever attended,' remarked a fan from Atlanta. 'It was more than worth the trip out to LA, to see the film, hear the talks and mostly to meet others devoted to the SS *United States* and the great liners!'

Myself, I am visiting the Cunard offices in Santa Clarita, California, on Monday, flying home on Tuesday and then heading off to distant Dubai on Friday. I join another ship, lecturing onboard for a month and all the way to London, and will be joined by a good friend, Robert Welding, whom I have not seen in 30 years. We'd met in Bermuda, where he was living, in 1970, but then 'lost touch', as they say, after he'd moved to Australia. Somehow, we were 'reunited' in February 2007, during a trip from San Francisco to Sydney aboard the *Queen Mary 2*. Himself, Bob Welding has a wealth of sea-going experience and recollection, having served aboard many ships, including the great Cunard liners, beginning in the late 1950s.

CUNARD REFLECTIONS & REMEMBRANCES

Liverpool-born and bred Bob Welding first went to sea in 1958 and then sailed aboard passenger ships until well into the late '60s. He served on the likes of the *Reina Del Mar, Britannic, Caronia, Sylvania* and the legendary *Queen Mary* and *Queen Elizabeth*.

He sailed to the Caribbean and South America, crossed the North Atlantic to New York as well as to Montreal and made three full world cruises. Dedication and lots of hard work, it was also romance, adventure and a young man's dreams come true. He was 15 when he first put to sea on the West Coast of South America-routed *Reina Del Mar* in 1958. 'It was a wonderful life for a relatively poor, working-class young man in 1950s Britain,' he said. 'It was a great opportunity. It was also totally exciting. Yes, it was lots of hard work, but I traveled everywhere. Family and friends back in Liverpool used to gather round and listen to my tales of faraway places.'

There were some 35,000 men and women working on the 2,000 ships of the British merchant navy in the late 1950s. Many went to sea to escape their home situation – and anything was more glamorous.

'Traveling the world seemed much more interesting than England at that time', remembered Welding. 'The wages at sea [$30 a month for an apprentice cook in 1959] were then one-third greater than those ashore and you actually could save money and possibly buy a house, a small one, of course. But you had to avoid the gambling amongst the crew. That could be deadly – all your wages gone even!

'Of course, going to sea was a wonderful opportunity to travel and see the world and meet different people and to buy things. Once, I came home with two Hawaiian shirts, all flowery and which were so unique in the UK back then. So, it was a chance to shop as well, to buy things such as portable radios, records in Manhattan and high-quality clothes. Many things were then affordable on a seaman's wages. I bought my first Fruit-of-the-Loom jockey shorts in New York for $1.50 for four in a packet. They were so much better than the old-fashioned, heavy cotton underpants we had in England. Fruit-of-the-Loom was very comfortable polished cotton.

'I was earning $30 a month in 1959, which was a decent wage in the UK then', he added. 'I could buy a lamb's wool sports jacket, trousers and shoes for $10. I felt very smart and very proud. 'I also had my Duffel coat [long top coat with a hood on top] bought from the Army & Navy Shop for my rovings around New York City. I also bought khaki trousers, which cost $2 a pair along Twelfth Avenue, but which were eye-openers back in England. I also bought jeans and soft moccasins. And I also got Pyrex pots and plates in New York. It was then $3 for three pots. Like me, many of the crew loved Woolworth's.'

Welding also served onboard the *Caronia* during her long cruises to ports all over the world, when purchases by the crew filled cabins and corridors. There would be carpets, those rattan chairs, and wooden chests.

'Our purchases, especially on the long cruises of the *Caronia*, filled crew cabins and corridors', he recalled. 'There were exotic carpets, chairs, wooden chests and carved tables. There was even a service that shipped the larger items direct from the ship at the Southampton Docks to your hometown in Britain. And those last few days on board were always so exciting. There was this great anticipation of going home – just being back in England. It was like the beginning of the long summer break from school.'

As an apprentice cook, Robert Welding rotated among many of the great Cunard liners of the day. He added, 'We worked almost the whole of the year on the *Caronia*. We had five weeks off out of fifty-two. You could take leave, of course, but it was best to stay with the ship, stick to the company schedule. Onboard the *Queen Mary* and *Queen Elizabeth*, it was three round trips to New York and back on and then one round trip off. As a cook, I lived in cabins that had two bunks, two stools, a washbasin, two wardrobes and a bare steel floor that was painted. They were actually very tight and quite dreary. A board was often placed over the washbasin and that created a table. There was forced-air ventilation, but – in lower-deck quarters – it was often difficult to sleep comfortably. The older liners absorbed more heat in port, as I remember, and so retained more heat and had less ventilation. On warm, summer nights, we slept on deck, on the forward hatch, on the old *Britannic*. A canvas tarp was put up and we brought up mattresses. On the *Caronia*, on her cruises in tropical waters, we slept in rattan lounge chairs under the countless stars of those warm nights.

'There was great shipboard discipline and rules at Cunard, of course. Every morning at 10, the crew quarters were inspected and checked for even the slightest dust. Of course, it was usually "Every "Every morning at 10, there were inspections of the crew quarters. Officers would check for the slightest dust. But those quarters were sweltering and dust was inevitable. Really, it was all about discipline and order. We knew, however, to avoid eye contact with the top officers and so not to be noticed. There was a Master-at-Arms that was usually either ex-Royal Navy or ex-police. There was a sort of little police station onboard and it included a lock-up somewhere, a kind of a brig.'

Bob last put to sea on a Cunard liner in the late 1960s, on the New York-to-Bermuda run aboard the *Franconia*. He later moved to Bermuda, then to Australia and later worked on Australian cargo vessels, tankers and even 'sugar boats'.

'Working on those early Cunard liners and others was sometimes a hard, sometimes even a lonely, isolating life, but it was also a wonderful life,' he concluded. 'The memories are treasures, absolute magic!'

Regal and majestic, the 1,132ft-long *Queen Mary 2* begins her passage along the Hudson River. (Cunard Line).

Left: Royal rendezvous in the North Atlantic. (Cunard Line).

Right: The Royal Air Force flypast escorts the *Queen Mary 2* as she nears the British coast. (Cunard Line).

Meeting of the *Queens* Down Under: the *QE2* is just arriving while the *Queen Mary* is berthed in the background in this view dated February 2007. (Cunard Line).

Left: Offering regular six-day crossings on the Atlantic between New York and Southampton, the *Queen Mary 2* passes the Lower Manhattan skyline. (Cunard Line).

Right: Heading out into the Atlantic, the 17-deck-high *Queen Mary 2* passes under New York's Verrazano-Narrows Bridge with a mere 14ft clearance. (Cunard Line).

Above left: Meeting at Port Everglades: the *Queen Mary 2* (left) and the *Queen Elizabeth 2* meet in the Florida port prior to departing on their respective world cruises, in a view dated January 2008. (Cunard Line).

Above right: Tight squeeze: The *Queen Mary 2* passes under the harbor bridge at Bergen, Norway, with only 9ft of clearance. This view dates from July 2004. (Cunard Line).

Left: The *Queen Mary 2* makes a nighttime departure from Hong Kong during the city's famed 'Symphony of Lights'. (Cunard Line).

Left: Maiden arrival at Le Havre on 24 July 2005. (Eric Houri Collection).

Right: Record-breaking day: eight cruise ships including the *Queen Mary* are together at Port Everglades in this 2005 view. (Port of Port Everglades Authority).

Above: The grand tandem departure of the two *Queens* from New York on April 25th 2004. (Cunard Line).

Left: The *Queen Mary 2* berthed at Red Hook, Brooklyn, in New York harbor. (Author's Collection).

Above left: Outbound from New York on May 30th 2007. (Ed Squire Collection).

Above right: Arriving at San Francisco for the first time in January 2007. (Author's Collection).

Right: Tropical setting: The *Queen Mary 2* berthed in the harbor on Pago Pago in the South Pacific. (Author's Collection).

Opposite left: Heavy seas: the *Queen Victoria* as seen from the *Queen Elizabeth 2* during the tandem transatlantic crossing in January 2008. (Cunard Line).

Opposite right: In reverse, the *QE2* as seen from the *Queen Victoria*, in January 2008. (Cunard Line).

Left: At Lisbon on June 24th 2008 with the Portugese naval vessel *Joao Roby* in the foreground. (Luis Miguel Correia Collection).

Right: The *Queen Victoria* (center) and the *Queen Elizabeth 2* (beyond) as seen from the aft decks of the *Queen Mary 2*, during the royal rendezvous in New York in January 2008. (Cunard Line).

Below: Heavy seas: the *Queen Elizabeth 2* as seen from the *Queen Victoria* during the tandem trans-Atlantic crossing in January 2008. (Cunard Line).

Bottom left: The *Queen Elizabeth 2* seen through the mist, in January 2008. (Cunard Line).

Bottom right: The *Queen Victoria* sails into the sun, January 2008. (Cunard Line).

Left: The *Queen Victoria* passing through the Panama Canal. (Cunard Line).

Left: The *Queen Mary 2* departing from New York with the Statue of Liberty resting on her upper decks. (Jeffrey Towns Collection).

Left: Double transit: The *Queen Victoria* passes through the locks of the Panama Canal with the 30,000-ton *Pacific Princess*. (Cunard Line).

Right: The *Queen Victoria* nears the Pacific Ocean as she completes her Panama Canal transit. (Cunard Line).

Left: The *Queen Victoria* has just passed under the Millenium Panama Canal Bridge. (Cunard Line).

Right: The *QE2* at New York with the *Crystal Symphony* on the right. (Robert O'Brien Collection)

At Lisbon on April 29th 2008. (Luis Miguel Correia Collection).

Another view at Lisbon. (Luis Miguel Correia Collection).

The *QE2* and the *Queen Mary 2* together at Port Everglades, Florida, in January 2008. (Cunard Line).

Left: Outbound on the Hudson. (Robert O'Brien Collection).

Right: Lifeboat drill at New York. (Robert O'Brien Collection).

Above left: Sailing from New York, April 2008. (Robert O'Brien Collection).

Above right: Misty afternoon at Southampton: the *QE2* with the *Pacific Princess* just behind in a view dated, April 22nd 2008. (Author's Collection).

Left: In the royal rendezvous at Southampton on April 22nd 2008, the *Queen Mary 2* approaches the *Queen Victoria*. (Cunard Line).

Above: The first meeting of the three *Queens* at Southampton created a special occasion. (Cunard Line).

Below: The QE2 as seen from the port-side bridge wing of the *Queen Mary 2*. (Author's Collection).

Largest of the three, the 1,132ft-long *Queen Mary 2* begins to turn for the 'sail past' of the QE2 and, farther beyond, the *Queen Victoria*. (Cunard Line).

Above left: The *Queen Mary 2* makes her precise turn. (Cunard Line).

Above right: The royal procession. (Cunard Line).

Left: Royal close-up! (Author's Collection).

Above: The three *Queens* with the *Queen Mary 2* placed nicely in the center. (Cunard Line).

Right: The *QE2*, minus some lifeboats as she undergoes 'wet dock' maintenance, as seen from the wheelhouse of the *Queen Mary 2*. (Author's Collection).

Above left: Another superb view of the three famed Cunarders. (Cunard Line).

Above right: Waiting for her moment of departure, the *Queen Victoria* was soon to sail off on a Mediterranean cruise. (Cunard Line).

Right: Great greetings were exchanged as the two ships passed one another. (Author's Collection).

Above: The *Queen Mary 2* begins to turn away, to begin her six-night transatlantic crossing to New York. (Cunard Line).

Right: The two newest Cunarders. (Cunard Line).

Below: The late afternoon sun silhouettes the three *Queens*. (Cunard Line).

Above and opposite page: The *QE2* and the *Queen Victoria* at Zeebrugge,
July 2008. (Cunard Line).

Above: A flotilla of small boats forms the royal escort. (Cunard Line).

Left: Her Majesty the Queen with no less than twelve Cunard captains, all of them masters at one time of the *QE2*. (Cunard Line).

OCTOBER 2008: FAREWELL VOYAGES ON THE QE2

Monday, 29 September

I'd flown from Newark to Heathrow the night before and, comparatively, a six-hour flight seems simple, easy, almost very short. We had the luxury of booking a car service, being met at the airport and then comfortably driven to Southampton and our hotel. A long morning rest was in order. Afterward, off to the waterfront to see that a new Ocean Terminal, but now as a very contemporary cruise terminal, is being constructed (sadly, the original, Deco-style Ocean Terminal, which was completed in 1950 but based on designs from the late '30s, was thoughtlessly demolished in 1983, only to become a scrap-metal depot).

Tuesday, 30 September

Board the majestic *QE2* at noon. A full house of loyalist passengers: older British types, many Americans too, a few ship enthusiasts. Happily, we are placed in a Deck Two Cabin, one of those roomy 'staterooms' with large beds, closets, sitting area and good-sized bathroom with a big, old-fashioned tub. Tea with Bea Muller, who has been 'living' aboard the ship for nine years and also with Irma and Doris, travel friends with thousands of Cunard days between them for their frequent sailor cards. Then dinner with Robert Lloyd, the superb, young maritime artist who has commissions to paint at least another one-hundred or so ships, many for rich Middle Eastern tanker owners.

We sail to a thunderous blowing of whistles – the *Artemis* (the former *Royal Princess*) goes out first and, as P&O Cruises is a sister company to Cunard in the vast Carnival-owned hierarchy, she comes very close to the *Elizabeth 2*, her decks and balconies crammed with onlookers. The impeccable, glistening *QE2* is of course very newsworthy in these final six weeks of sea-going service before going to Dubai and a gentile retired life as a moored hotel, entertainment center and museum (the latest word is still, by the way, that mega-rich Dubai want to gut and then rebuild and restore her innards in the original, '60s, Twiggy-era stylings and décor).

Above left: Farewell season: the *QE2* at historic Liverpool. (Charles Cotton Collection).

Above right: The last entry to the River Clyde. (Author's Collection).

Left: The farewell visit to Greenock, October 2008. (Author's Collection).

Above left: Rainy day at Belfast, October 2008. (Author's Collection).

Above right: Final call at Liverpool as seen from the roof of the Cunard Building. (Author's Collection).

Right: The author atop the Cunard Building at Liverpool. The famed Royal Liver Building is in the background. (Author's Collection).

Above left: The last hammerhead crane, now a tourist attraction, at the former John Brown Shipyard at Clydebank. (Author's Collection).

Above right: Starboard side view of the *Queen Mary 2* during the tandem crossing. (Charles Cotton Collection).

Left: Final tandem crossing: the *Queen Mary 2* as seen from the *QE2*, October 2008. (John McFarland Collection).

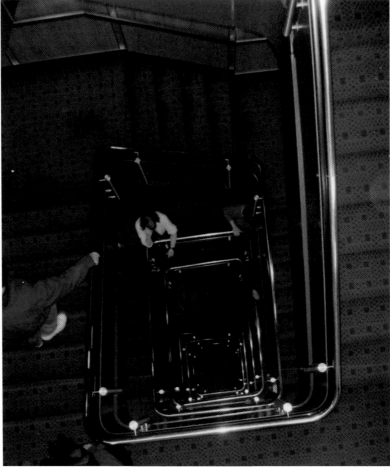

Above left: A stairwell view. (Charles Cotton Collection).

Above right: A poetic view from one *Queen* to another! (Charles Cotton Collection).

Right: Interesting perspective: one of the stairwells aboard the *QE2*. (Charles Cotton Collection).

Above left: The open Promenade Deck aboard the *QE2*. (Charles Cotton Collection).

Above right: The *Queen Mary 2* says goodbye to the *QE2* at sea in a view dated October 21st 2008. (Charles Cotton Collection).

Left: Farewell to New York: the *QE2* heads down the Hudson River for the very last time. (Robert O'Brien Collection).

Opposite top: At Southampton, ready to leave on her penultimate voyage, the *QE2*'s funnel is set off by the Stothert & Pitt-constructed dockside crane. (Campbell McCutcheon).

Opposite bottom: The *QE2* berthed at Lisbon on her second-but last entry to the port. (Campbell McCutcheon).

Far right: The 40-ton crane at the *QE2* terminal would be hard-pressed to lift the *QE2*'s majestic funnel. (Campbell McCutcheon).

QUEEN ELIZABETH2
FAREWELL SEASON
OFFICERS & CREW
7 SEPTEMBER 2008

Best Wishes,
John Duffy
Hotel Manager QE2
1981 – 2008

Left: Despite their sheer size, few modern cruise ships can compare with the flowing lines of the *QE2*'s bow or the majesty of her bridge front. (Campbell McCutcheon).

Below: With major use of aluminum on her upper decks, the *QE2*'s lines are uncluttered by the rivets and steel plates so visible on her two older sisters, *Queen Mary* and *Queen Elizabeth*. (Campbell McCutcheon).

Opposite far left: Sardinia, November 1st 2008. (Campbell McCutcheon).

Above left: With ominous black clouds rolling overhead, and flying the flag of Italy while berthed at Cagliari, the heavens were to open later and drench the many passengers ashore. (Campbell McCutcheon).

Left: During the farewell season for the *QE2*, the officers and crew pose on the foredeck of the ship in a photo dated 7 September 2008. (Cunard Line).

Messina, November 3rd 2008. The most noticable element of a British ocean liner is the expanse of deck area at the stern, complete with swimming pool, lido and open space. (Campbell McCutcheon).

Above: Viewed from one of the many ferries plying their trade from Sicily to the toe of Italy, the *QE2* shimmers against the blue Sicilian skies. (Campbell McCutcheon).

Right: Perhaps the cheapest photographic platform in the world, the ferry from Messina costs but €1, but affords the most glorious views of visiting ships. (Campbell McCutcheon).

This page: Destroyed by an earthquake in 1908, bombed by the Allies during the invasion of Italy in 1943, Messina is hardly a pretty city, but the backdrop of mountains which encompass the city add to the majesty of the scene on the *QE2*'s final call to the Italian island. (Campbell McCutcheon).

Opposite page: The *QE2*'s lines compared with those of the new breed of cruise ship, in this case Royal Caribbean's *Brilliance of the Seas*, one of two RCL ships she was to encounter on her penultimate voyage. (Campbell McCutcheon).

Left: Rising above a sea of containers, the stern of the *QE2* at the maritime terminal in Naples, November 2008. (Campbell McCutcheon).

Below: The Bridge wing of the *QE2*. (Campbell McCutcheon).

Opposite page: The funnel of the *QE2* (Campbell McCutcheon)

These pages: With two tender ports, the *QE2*'s penultimate cruise would be the last opportunity for passengers to see the majesty of the *QE2*. Here at Dubrovnik, the gem of the Adriatic, and sadly shelled during the civil war, the *QE2* shows her lines off under blue skies. (Campbell McCutcheon).

Opposite page: Swinging on her starboard anchor, the bow of the QE2 is showing signs of a hard summer of cruises and transatlantic crossings. Weatherworn, she would be painted again before her final departure from Southampton. (Campbell McCutcheon).

Above and right: Tenders swarming around her, the QE2's size is clear. (Campbell McCutcheon).

Left: Passenger tender no.9 approaches the harbor at Dubrovnik. (Campbell McCutcheon).

Below: The hills around Dubrovnik afford some fantastic views of ships anchored off the walled city. (Campbell McCutcheon).

Opposite page: With her high cruising speed, the *QE2* can travel to many ports impossible for other cruise ships to reach in a two-week cruise from Southampton. Here, at Piraeus, the port of Athens, she is being refueled for the final journey back to her homeport. Piraeus provided the spectacle of the last two Clyde-built ocean liners in port together for the last time, when *Mona Lisa*, the ex-Swedish Amerika Line's *Kungsholm*, and a firm favourite as *Sea Princess* and as *Victoria* for P&O, called into the port on a Peace Boat charter. (Campbell McCutcheon).

Opposite page and above: Thomson Spirit, originally the 1983-built *Nieuw Amsterdam*, was in Piraeus too. (Campbell McCutcheon).

Right: The distinctive funnel of the *QE2*. (Campbell McCutcheon).

Opposite page and above: Piraeus is one of the busiest harbours in the Mediterranean, and a lot of ship-repair work is done here. *Thomson Spirit* leaves, empty, for a refit. (Campbell McCutcheon).

Right: QE2 Crew Only! (Campbell McCutcheon).

Opposite page: The sun sets on the *QE2*'s final day in Piraeus. (Campbell McCutcheon)

Right: Halloween aboard. This grizzly sight awaited those brave enough to venture into the Lido restaurant. (Campbell McCutcheon).

Bottom right: After-dinner drinks involved negotiating past the witches in the Yacht Club. (Campbell McCutcheon).

Above: Gibraltar was sunny and it was time for some final painting before the return to Southampton for the 11th. Two brave deck crew are lowered to paint the rust-stained area around the ship's starboard anchor. (Campbell McCutcheon).

Left: The return to Southampton was on 11 November, Remembrance Day, and QE2's flag flew at half-mast as the departing passengers disembarked and her final sea-going passengers began to arrive. (Campbell McCutcheon).

Above: At 11am, two aircraft flew over and dropped thousands of poppies over the *QE2*. (Campbell McCutcheon).

Right: With the car-carrier *Pacific Spirit* to her stern, a ceremony was held as the flag was lowered. Because of her stranding on a sandbank earlier that morning, some passengers were lucky enough to remain onboard for this poignant reminder of soldiers lost in two World Wars and numerous conflicts since. (Campbell McCutcheon).

RESIDENT OF THE SEAS: BEA MULLER

When Bea Muller first went to sea little more than 15 years ago, then a virtual novice to ocean liners, she and her late husband made the 95-day world cruise of the *QE2*. But she was soon 'hooked' – and 'line and sinker' too! Now 89, she has been 'living' aboard the iconic *Queen Elizabeth 2* for the past nine years. She is, without question, the current world champ of cruise loyalists. Back in the 1950s, the late Clara MacBeth lived aboard another Cunard liner, the legendary *Caronia*, the famed 'Green Goddess' of long, luxurious cruising, for 14 years.

The subject of almost countless TV and radio interviews, newspaper and magazine articles, featured in maritime books and herself a segment star on television's news weekly *Sixty Minutes*, Bea has been madly in love with the legendary *QE2* and has sailed on hundreds of voyages. The ship is indeed the old, long-serving sailor (39 years in all and more records than any other big liner in history) has gone off to a new life out in Dubai, where she will be renovated as a luxury hotel and nautical museum while moored on the extravagant Palm Island. Bea was, of course, aboard for the final hours, seeing the Cunard and the British flags hauled down and the official signing over to her new Middle Eastern owners. 'I'm heartsick, of course,' said the energetic Bea, an official resident of Somerville in central New Jersey, but then something of an 'international citizen'. We sailed together, in the wake of many prior trips together, just last October – on true sentimental journeys, the *Elizabeth*'s 'Farewell to the British Isles' cruise and then the Last Westbound Crossing to New York.

'The *QE2* has been my home off and on, but mostly on, for the past 14 years – nine years full-time!' she said with a proud smile as we sipped and ate our way through one of those elegant, white glove teas in the splendors of the Queens Room aboard the 70,000-ton *Elizabeth 2*. 'There is no ship like the *QE2* and there never, ever will be again,' she added nostalgically. 'But now, I have to find a new home. I am going to cry a lot. But I am going next [in December] to the *Queen Victoria*, for a Mediterranean cruise, and try to "live" at 21 knots (the ever-powerful *QE2* could, when pushed, top 32 knots) and then on the 100-night world cruise of the *Queen Mary 2*. But mostly, I will miss the wonderful personnel and fellow passengers aboard the *QE2*. We were like a family. And the *QE2* gave me up to forty-eight ports of call each year. Yes, I will miss the *QE2*. Sadly, nothing is forever!'

Tuesday, 30 September

Stormy seas predicted tonight for the Channel and so tomorrow's call at Cherbourg over in France has been canceled already and instead this otherwise strong, very sturdy liner (like a battleship!) will head west and dock in Cobh in Ireland a day early and so an unexpected overnight stop there. But well into night, the 70,000-ton, 963ft-long QE2 creaks and moans. Hugely efficient, the cruise staff create a full day (Wednesday) of activities. My first lecture is brought forward and also then a book signing outside the library. Signing pens ready! Lights, camera, action (and of course make-up) at 10 tomorrow morning!

While reading late tonight, I discover that Herr Hitler was planning to use Windsor Castle as his headquarters after his planned, storm-trooper-filled invasion of Britain in the summer of 1940.

Wednesday, 1 October

A rolling Queen as we sail westward to Ireland. 'The Irish Sea is kicking-up', as one waiter says. The arrival in Cobh (Cork) is pushed up to 1 o'clock. A few grim faces, however, at breakfast. 'I didn't sleep a wink last night', said a man from Slough in England who is on his very first voyage.

Power meal! Unexpected breakfast with Carol Marlow, president of Cunard, who is so totally unpretentious – she waits and carries a tray in the Lido and then fetches her own coffee. She tells me that everything will go with the QE2 to Dubai and which 'makes her completely Cunard', as she puts it. Only a few items, such as the royal penants, on loan from the Queen herself, will be returned. She also mentions that the new Queen Elizabeth, due out in October 2010, will cruise on a worldwide scope including New York sailings. Later, she attends my first lecture, sitting in the second row and afterward, in great kindness, called it 'the most fantastic, most wonderful lecture she'd ever heard!' Well, I guess that means I can have that extra dessert. (Carol Marlow leaves this trip on Friday, in Liverpool, but will be aboard the very final voyage from Southampton to Dubai, but boarding at Alexandria in Egypt. Indeed, she's a very busy lady.)

After my first talk, there are always stories and recollections: a Canadian lady tells me of her wartime passage in the French *Pasteur,* sailing from Liverpool to New York in 1941 ('Sometimes we hid under dining room tables if there was a U-boat alert,' she remembered); another talks of a 1949 trip to New Zealand aboard the *Rangitiki* ('The most awful old tub,' she says); and still another of emigrating to New York on the *Queen Mary* in 1946. Afterward, an hour-long book signing outside the ship's

library and, happily, altogether we sell 112 books. Alone, one man bought six copies of the new QE2 picture book from Dover and also we told six copies of the big, heavy, $65-a-copy *Liners of the Golden Age* book.

Reunion with Captain Robin Woodall, now in his 80s and traveling as a passenger, but a grand gentleman who started with Cunard in 1950 and was master of the *Cunard Countess* in Nov '83 when we cruised the Eastern Caribbean together. We also had the most wonderful one-on-one interview on an otherwise fog-filled westbound crossing of this ship back in Aug '93.

The BBC News is less than comforting: hideous financial problems not only in the United States, but seemingly spreading everywhere, to Europe, even the Far East. The American House of Representatives has voted down a $700 billion bailout plan, the real estate market seems to have slipped further into a deep freeze and banks on both sides of the great Atlantic seem to be collapsing.

Mid-afternoon arrival at Cobh in Ireland, the once booming port that saw millions of immigrants head mostly for American shores and, now more notably than ever, the last stop for the infamous *Titanic* on that otherwise doomed maiden voyage back in Apr 1912. We are a day early, and so the little waterside shops busily stock shelves, enrich front window displays, add staff. This now small port (although visited by about 50 cruise ships per year these days) is quaintly charming: row houses, curved streets, little lanes, the likes of the Lusitania Pub and then a Mauretania Pub as well, a ten-seat Chinese restaurant and, looming above, in a great Gothic stone tribute to the Almighty reaching for the Heavens, atop a hill, the lean 400ft spire of St Fin Barre's Cathedral.

Night aboard: formal wear and so everything in full force including glistening rhinestones, gold and silver sandal shoes, a few prominent decorations and medals, and even a Ginger Rogers-like white-fox stole. There's a ball in the Queens Room and the dancing, with the British mostly, is in full force. Paul Ritchie, an old friend and the lead singer for the so-called QE2 orchestra, is better than ever. Great charm, high-voltage energy and an enriched voice!

Thursday, 3 October

Walk into Cobh and discover the former Cunard and White Star Line offices, now in re-use of course, and then a small hotel along the seafront with a brass plaque stating 'former passenger offices of the United States Lines'. Then a pause in St Fin Barre's – a prayer and some reflective time peering at the many glorious stained-glass windows highlighted by a background of blazing sunlight. An Irish male chorus sings in the background and all while the ornate main altar is specially floodlit on this day in honor of the *QE2*'s final visit. Hundreds, or so it seems, of blue-suited elementary school kids seem to be everywhere, pads in hand and sketching the monstrously high *Queen*. I can't help but look over a few little shoulders and see the early images. In fading autumn light, in a sort of misty pink, thousands later cram the waterfront, rooftops and hillsides to see us sail at 6:00pm. Farewell great *Queen*!

Friday, 4 October

Morning in the Irish Sea, bound for historic Liverpool. But news from home, mostly via BBC and Sky on television, is weird, strange, confusing, but certainly worrisome! The financial situation remains like the *Andrea Doria*: struck, mortally wounded, sinking hard and fast! Values decreasing and declining everywhere, so it seems. Reports of a lady (in Saginaw, Michigan), for example, who, in an extreme example of course, just bought a house, a small one, at auction for $1.75. Here in England, Howard tells me that local newspapers are running full-page ads: 'Sell your gold and jewelry and other valuables to raise cash!' All beginning to sound like Wall Street in October 1929! But, in great juxtaposition, aboard this classic, always newsy palace of the seas, we seem to worry more about items on the dinner menu and the nighttime offerings in the daily program and, perhaps in the slightest touch of reality, whether or not it will rain in, say, Liverpool!

Morning talk by Captain Robin Woodall, with Cunard since 1950, former master of the *QE2* and now in his 80s. Most articulate, he recounts many stories, some quite enlightening. 'The Queen Mother was due to attend and participate in Cunard's 150th-anniversary ceremonies and short, celebratory cruise on the *QE2* from Spithead up to Southampton, in July 1990,' he told us. 'But then, it all caught the Queen's eye and she reportedly phoned her mother and said: "Mummy, I think I will do that event. I've never sailed aboard the *QE2* and, after all, she is *my ship*!"'

Chats with three interesting ladies, indeed women of the seas: Rose Everett, now about 90, is on her 200th or maybe 300th cruise. She can't quite remember, so she says. A friend from New York, she tells me of Paris and her studying fashion there in the late 1940s and early '50s ... and of her classmates, namely Yves St Laurent and Pierre Cardin. Decades later, she 'borrows' Pierre's penthouse in Beijing (well, for a few nights anyway) and tells of its lighted glass floors, huge art collection and of the three rooms that joined together formed the 'bathroom'. Shirley Matchett was

my tablemate on a cruise to Rio, aboard the *Queen Mary 2* in Feb '06, and has that wonderful, free, life-loving, ever-cheerful Australian flair to her personality. There are no pretentions; she reminds me (in speech, anyway) of the infamous Dame Edna and now has a different beau (this one from Texas and all while she herself lives in far-off Melbourne). Then there's Denny Farmer, widow of a legendary Cunard chief engineer and herself a veteran traveler of hundreds of voyages, who was presented to the Queen during the royal farewell visit and lunch to the *QE2* last June. Seems Her Majesty especially enjoyed chatting and, for several minutes, asked about Denny's favorite ports, the names of the ships she sailed and how she felt about the *Elizabeth 2* going to Dubai. But Denny wanted to finish it all on a high note and so said to the smiling sovereign, 'I'm looking forward very much to the *next Queen Elizabeth*!' Her Majesty suddenly looked puzzled, then frowned, but then giggled. 'You mean the ship, of course!' she said as she straightened that ever-present handbag and moved on.

Hotel director and longtime friend John Duffy, with Cunard for 43 years, tells me that he has now decided not to retire after the *QE2* arrives in Dubai and instead will transfer to the *Queen Victoria*. Another old friend, a bedroom steward, who joined Cunard 45 years ago and who looked after the likes of Elizabeth Taylor, is also staying on and transferring to either the *Mary 2* or the *Victoria*.

Liverpool off the port bow: a midday, 12 noon arrival and we berth at the year-old cruise terminal created along the old Princes Landing Stage, the famed passenger-ship dock.

A gloriously memorable day, blessed by brisk but sun-filled autumn weather ... in fact, at times that wonderfully unique-to-these-British-Isles weather of often immense, silver-lined cloud formations above and lemony, very bright, almost harsh sunlight below. The glows and shadowings, especially on period brick and stone buildings, especially the melancholy, Victorian-era warehouses, is absolute magic. After being eased into that new Liverpool Cruise Terminal, we meet dear John Heywood, a friend of some 30 years down by car from Lancaster, and then off we go: seven hours of adventure, information, fresh scenery – first to the former Cunard Building and the company headquarters (1916-68), where we are given a behind-the-scenes tour (to the former grand lounge for waiting first-class passengers, to the lower basements where luggage was stored and the third-class immigrants processed and finally up on the roof, just below the flagpoles where some tests were run in planning for the legendary *Queen Mary* in the early 1930s; then to the mostly desolate docklands, with more of those sentimental warehouses and now empty docks with names such as Huskisson, Gladstone & Canada, and where the great liners once berthed in between trans-ocean crossings; then to the marshes and on to the golden sands up at Crosby (and as a freighter departs in silhouetted, late-afternoon light); then to the row houses of Waterloo, which includes the rather grand former home of the Ismay family, the owners of the famed White Star Line, and from the rooftop of which they watched the likes of the *Teutonic* sail off to far-away America back in the 1880s; then to the Albert Dock, the Maritime Museum and a late, late lunch at the Gusto Restaurant (and where we were just last July); then through a much revitalized, rebuilt downtown (gleaming mega malls, to say the least); then to the famed Adelphi Hotel (once used by first-class transatlantic passengers and also a set piece in the classic *Brideshead Revisited* television series); then to both cathedrals, first the Catholic with its crown-like tower and then to the huge, very ponderous Anglican one, but with the most imposing, inspiring, almost diminishing innards; then, and now after dark, driving through the old backstreets, moodful warehouse districts and through neon-glittering Chinatown. We return to the *QE2* in time for sailing at 10. The dock is crammed with thousands, those thunderous whistles sound and echo across the famed Mersey and they signal the start of colorful fireworks. Afterward, we cast off: sentimental music, the docks thick with passengers and crew, that hearty whistle sounding and acknowledging the farewell toots of other craft.

Saturday, 5 October

Fame and celebrity are indeed fleeting. Saw John Prescott, former Deputy Prime Minister under Tony Blair, fetching his own coffee in the Lido. Later, introduced to Sir Jimmy Saville, now in his 80s and unassumingly wearing an otherwise unremarkable jogging suit, but who is evidently a hugely well-known and successful TV and radio personality in the UK. He is always alone as he strolls the ship. And journalist Carol Thatcher, daughter of the illustrious Margaret, was aboard the last three days and just about came and went unnoticed and unannounced. Then Commodore Ron and Kim Warwick (he was, of course, the very popular master of the *QE2* and *QM2*) boarded yesterday at Liverpool, waiting at the gangway, then finally boarded unescorted and all but carried their own luggage.

Jim Carlisle meets us in Belfast this afternoon. While he works on oil rigs off in the North Sea and is an ocean liner enthusiast, his father worked for the local Harland & Wolff shipyard (located just across from the *QE2*, here today on her simultaneous first and last visit to this capital of Northern Ireland) for 51 years. But it was indeed a different era, a long bygone age. He worked six days a week, peddled nine miles each way to and from the yard and was given only a seven-minute bathroom break each day. Earlier, Jim's grandfather had helped build the immortal *Titanic* while his father worked on hundreds of ships including such noted liners as the *Southern Cross* and *Canberra*. We visit the old workshops, slipways, the long-empty graving dock used by the *Titanic* herself. In the café in the old pump house, we run aground a trio of long-retired shipyard workers, gathered round cups of tea and deep in recollections. One of them, who started at Harland & Wolff during the Second World War, in 1942, proudly tells me, 'I still have my ticket to the launching by the Queen of the *Southern Cross* [August 1954]. That day, the rains never ceased.' Another reminds me that actually three Belfast-built ships sank on their maiden voyages. 'There was the *Titanic* in 1912, of course, and then the *Magdalena* [a passenger-cargo liner belonging to the Royal Mail Lines] in 1949,' he tells me with the relish of revealing a great secret. 'The third ship was a freighter belonging to the Clan Line.' The weather here today is so moodful: chilly rain, fog, the *QE2* across the harbor all but disappearing at times in the mists. Indeed, Belfast is a city that echoes enormous shipping and shipbuilding history.

Robert Lloyd tells me at dinner that his great artistic skills are quite diverse. Apart from painting ships of every kind, shape and size, in his early days he was responsible for the logo of Virgin Atlantic Airlines.

After dinner, I meet a former engineer, who sailed with the Anchor Line on the old run between Liverpool, the Suez and Bombay. 'I served [in the late 1950s] in the *Cilicia*, which was a wonderful old ship and which was like a floating club with only 300 all-first-class passengers', he tells me. 'She had unremarkable, but the most exquisitely maintained quarters. Everything was polished and scrubbed. We carried lots of the old contract tea planters and merchants, some government officials, the odd tourist and, on occasion, even Indian royalty. I remember one of the maharanees traveling up to England. She'd come to dinner in shimmering silks, ropes of pearls and jewel-encrusted slippers.'

Sunday, 6 October

Morning lecture by John Whitworth, managing director of Cunard in the 1960s during the creation and construction of the *QE2*. He offers some interesting and enlightening insights.

QE2: THE EARLY YEARS …

John Whitworth, now retired and in his 80s and living in the idyllic English countryside, was a director and later, at the very top of the bosun's ladder, the managing director of the great, hugely historic Cunard Line in 1960s. In 1965, the company was still the largest – if not the busiest – on the North Atlantic run. 'Getting there was still half the fun' – if less and less appealing on five- to eight-day ocean liner crossings.

There were the iconic *Queens*, the original *Queen Mary* (completed in 1936) and the *Queen Elizabeth* (sent to sea for the first time just as the Second World War began, in 1940) as well as the *Mauretania, Caronia, Carmania, Franconia, Carinthia* and *Sylvania*. But time was running out – and running out all too quickly – as the decisive airlines and their jet liners drew more and more passengers and had Cunard losing over $5 million a year. Crossings were all but over and cruising was the future. But while the *Queen Mary* was retired in 1967, Cunard planned – and with great, if misguided hopes – that a new Atlantic superliner could be built to sail (at least until, in the then far-off future of 1975) in weekly tandem with the aging, but refitted *Queen Elizabeth*. The new liner project, a creation of early '60s enthusiasm, was dubbed the *Q3* project.

'We had our first meetings in October 1961 to plan for the *Q3*, the replacement for the then 25-year-old *Queen Mary*,' recalled John Whitworth. 'Cunard was then still a very conservative, very British, very old-fashioned company,' he added. 'Their Liverpool headquarters was a commercial palace and was dubbed "the Kremlin" by everyone in middle management. Top management was absolutely dictatorial. But the *Q3* was the wrong design – she was a rather traditional ship in many ways. The British side of Cunard wanted two classes whereas, rather unexpectedly, the New York office still pushed for the traditional three classes: first, cabin and tourist. The whole idea and the entire design were soon scrapped, quite fortunately.

'The *Q3* design was redone and became the *Q4*, which in turn became the *Queen Elizabeth 2*. The British government, after much wooing by Cunard, provided a $60 million loan. Shipyards began to bid after the design was announced in December 1962. John Brown on the Clyde in Scotland got the order, with some politics in play as well, and this was made public on December 30th 1964. [Among others, John Brown's yard had built the likes of the *Lusitania, Aquitania* and both the *Queen Mary* and *Queen Elizabeth*.]

'Plans for the new *Q4* were reworked and then reworked again and again,' he continued. 'At the same time, there was new, fresh management coming aboard at Cunard. The dust was gradually blown away and a new team of 40-year-olds were in place. There was even a new, enlightened, very contemporary design team. Captain William Warwick was appointed the first master of the new ship [65,000 tons at estimates of the day] and the plan to operate with the older, but larger *Elizabeth* were in place. But there was a devastating British maritime strike in May and June of 1966. Cruelly, it lasted six weeks and, like others, Cunard lost millions, in fact something close to $15 million. And, as the jet liners made deeper inroads, plans were changed – the old *Elizabeth* was out [and sold off in 1968] and the new *Q4* would operate in tandem with a former competitor, the French Line, and their four-year-old *France*.'

John Whitworth was placed in charge of selling off the 31-year-old *Queen Mary* in 1967 and the 28-year-old *Elizabeth* the following year. Faded and rusting, they were still two of the most famous liners ever built and while the 83,673-ton *Elizabeth* was still the largest liner yet to go to sea.

'I sold the much-loved *Queen Mary* for $3½ million in cash to the City of Long Beach in California,' he recounted. 'The *Queen Elizabeth* went a year later, but for $7½ million to Philadelphia buyers, mostly on credit. Cunard lost lots of money on that transaction.' [The 1,031ft-long *Elizabeth* later found her way to Fort Lauderdale, then being auctioned-off to Chinese buyers in 1970, but only to burn and sink in Hong Kong harbor in Jan 1972.]

The *Q4* was now, in 1967, well under construction along the famed River Clyde. 'Cunard was quite desperate in the summer of 1967, even a month before the ship's scheduled launching. We did not have enough money to continue,' added John Whitworth. 'We all but had to "beg" the British Government for further assistance, more loans. On September 14th, just six days before the actual launching, the Board of Trade agreed. They gave us the monies. The formal naming by Her Majesty the Queen would take place on the 20th. All seemed well, at least for the moment.'

By 1967, and much like some new laundry detergent or aerosol deodorant, Cunard wanted a new image, a new look, something away from the sometimes staid and dowdy era of the perceived traditional, stuffy Cunard and the wood-paneled, almost dowdy-by-then era of the original, 1930s-style *Queen Mary* and *Queen Elizabeth*. Now, it was the 'new Britain' – the age of Carnaby Street, Twiggy, James Bond and Formica. Cunard had to be like, well London, and start to swing. After all, it was the new age of floating hotels, classless ships and a different kind of competition with the fiercely competitive and immensely successful airlines. Due to be launched on 20 September 1967 at the John Brown Shipyard at Clydebank in Scotland and to be royally baptized by none other than Her Majesty Queen Elizabeth II, the ship's actual name was still top secret. There had been all sorts of rumors about: *British Queen*, *Princess Anne*, *Britannia*, even *Winston Churchill*, *William Shakespeare* and *John F. Kennedy*.

'Secretly, it had been decided [earlier in 1967] by Cunard's top management that the ship would be named *Queen Elizabeth*,' remembered John Whitworth. 'We prepared a sealed envelope for the Queen as she reached the podium on the launching day. But she refused to accept it and decided to proceed with the naming. She called the ship *Queen Elizabeth the Second*. Well, we were all very surprised, even shocked. She did not mean *Queen Elizabeth II* as she is only Elizabeth II of England, but not of Scotland and so that would have been quite, well, politically incorrect. So, we decided rather quickly on *Queen Elizabeth 2* and, almost immediately, we had the acronym of *QE2*.'

The crowds – shipyard officials, workers and their families and invited guests – cheered as the 963ft-long liner went down the ways. 'There were great clouds of red smoke as she slid down the ways, but in ways possibly an omen of troubled times ahead for the new liner,' recalled John Whitworth. 'She cost as much as 17 times more than projected and was soon bedeviled with strikes, work stoppages and – embarrassingly – huge pilferages. Sometimes, more new doors and furnishings and fresh carpets were going out of the shipyard than coming in. Then there were mechanical problems. The first trials [in Nov 1968] had to

be aborted because of an oil leak. A planned Christmas cruise [to the Canary Islands from Southampton] had to be canceled. Then there were electrical problems. Even though she managed a very impressive 32.4-knot top speed on successive trial runs, she had seemingly countless defects and deficiencies. We sent her to the Canaries on a shakedown cruise with Cunard guests only, a sort of trial run, but then there were further turbine troubles. She limped into Las Palmas in all but disgrace [on December 28th]. Cunard refused acceptance of the ship.

'This was, of course, a big blow to our planning, our scheduling, our high-spirited and very expensive advertising and marketing for the maiden season in 1969. British newspapers were quite ruthless and one of them dubbed her "the Ship of Shame" in a blazing headline.'

Repairs and corrections took months. The maiden voyage for Jan 1969 was canceled and rescheduled several times. 'She was like Terminal 5 at Heathrow in 2008 and had all sorts of problems in the beginning,' he concluded. 'Finally, in March, we had the perfect trials and the perfect delivery. We took aboard our first fare-paying passenger on April 22nd. The Queen visited the ship [at Southampton] on May 1st and Cunard management seemed pleased, proud, full of smiles. Now, a newspaper dubbed her "the Ship for All Seasons". But even after she set off for New York on her very first crossing and for a long time afterward, skepticism in the UK lingered. She was often called a "white elephant". But happily, she earned nearly $5 million in her first year. Now, in 2008, she has endured for 39 years and has been the success, even through some further hardships and hard times, that we had hoped for back in the '60s.'

As a last remark, John Whitworth added, 'I am glad that the *QE2* is going to Dubai. She will be preserved. Her future is great, even exciting!'

Sunday, 5 October

Midday arrival at Greenock, the port in western Scotland for Glasgow and mouth of the famed River Clyde. Scotland was once the shipbuilding capital of the world. Until the '60s, there were as many as 55 shipyards along the Clyde. Today, there are three, all of them smaller and very specialized. In the most perfect, almost warm weather, we arrive in late morning: horns honking, flags fluttering, hundreds of small boats serenading the great *QE2*, the last big liner to be built here in Scotland and along the Clyde. Alec and Mhairi Laing, dear friends from many visits here, take us out to the site of the former John Brown shipyard, where many, many ships were created including, of course, the *Queen Mary* and *Queen Elizabeth* and then, in the late 1960s, the *QE2*. Closed in the '90s and now all but gone completely, one great component remains: the 1907-built Titan hammerhead crane. Preserved and refurbished, it is now a tourist attraction and so we go to the top, walk out on the lifting arm and watch a video in the original cab. The views in all directions are spectacular. One of the guides worked at John Brown's for 40 years. 'I helped to build the bow of the *QE2*,' he tells us with smiling pride.

Afterward, tea with the Laings at their delightful home in Port Glasgow, perched high above the river and with a long terrace for panoramic views. The *QE2* is off in the distance, glistening in the late afternoon sun, and all while five Royal Navy warships wait offshore at anchor.

Onboard, there are many day visitors – including Gordon Bauwens, the very splendid maritime artist from Edinburgh who has unveiled his excellent rendition of the three Cunard *Queens*.

We sail at 10 – to countless flashing cameras, bagpipers along the dock, the ship's booming whistles and to another gala set of cascading fireworks. The last great liner to be built in Scotland was leaving Scotland for the very last time. Yes, there were some tears.

Monday, 6 October

A gray, sometimes misty morning as the *QE2* rounds the very northern tip of Scotland. A day onboard floating about as usual – from meal to meal, activity to activity. Cmdr Warwick kicks off at 10 with a lecture on the ship's heroic role during the 1982 Falklands War, then it's the choral director of Liverpool Cathedral and, by afternoon, Carol Thatcher on her life and times, but mostly with her illustrious mother.

Weekend BBC news is varied: Prince Charles has announced that he will give Balmoral Castle, dating from Queen Victoria's era, to the government of Scotland for use as, among other things, a conference center when he

becomes king; Wendy Richard, the blonde actress best remembered as Miss Brahms from the 1970s TV series *Are You Being Served* and later as the long-suffering Pauline in the British soap *EastEnders*, has disclosed that she is dying with fast-spreading cancer at age 65; and the financial situation, now a daily headline, is worsening quickly throughout these British Isles.

Tuesday, 7 October

Rather interesting statistic – 40 per cent of the 1,690 passengers aboard this trip are first-time *QE2* travelers and many of them first timers with Cunard. 'I just had to make a trip on her,' commented a man in his 80s from Southampton. 'I've never sailed on anything bigger than a Channel ferry.' Another added, 'My father went to sea with Cunard in the 1930s, aboard the *Andania*, and so I feel connected to him on this, my own first voyage with Cunard. And of course, it is very special because the *QE2* is a great symbol of British might and determination, design and engineering – and, in ways, a last symbol of what seems to be a bygone nation.'

A Canadian lady with a heavily flowered hat said, 'I emigrated from Southampton on the *Saxonia* in 1955 and then returned several years later to see my family on the *Ivernia*. Then I went back home to Canada on the *Carinthia* and, in later years, I've made a dozen trips on the *QE2*. I feel a very close kinship to Cunard.' A man from Newcastle added, 'I worked as a seaman for Cunard some 50 years ago, but only on the freighters. I sailed on the *Assyria*, *Asia*, *Alsatia*, *Andria* and *Bactria*. We always heard about the glamour and great style of the Cunard liners. It has taken me 50 years to sail on a passenger ship and I feel one of the last voyages of the great *QE2* is a perfect start and, at my age [92], possibly the perfect ending as well.'

Lunch with Commodore Warwick, his wife Kim, Doug Ward (the noted cruise critic and author) and John Duffy, the ship's longtime hotel director. Later, I ask to photograph Bea Muller, who has been 'living' aboard for nine years. 'I normally charge $10, but it is $5 for you,' she says with a chuckle.

Rainy, moodful Edinburgh … ship anchored just outside the famed Forth Bridge at South Queensferry and, even with her 963ft, she swings with the strong tide. Michael goes into town and, despite today's rail strike, finds his way back to the ship, even walking through darkened woods from the rail station near Queensferry itself and then down 100 stone steps to the little village and the tender berth. Harrier jets as a sail-off treat are obscured by the heavy gray clouds, but fireboats sprout and other boats signal with whistles and sirens as the very last great liner built in Scotland leaves home waters for the very last time.

'I'm very happy to be aboard this sentimental, Farewell to the British Isles cruise,' said a lady from Southport, near Liverpool. 'But sometimes, especially when that whistle sounds, I am close to tears.'

Wednesday, 8 October

My first visit to Newcastle, well rejuvenated these days but much changed. The famed 'coals from Newcastle' are now imported, in fact as much as 90 per cent from Poland. And the last of the famous shipyards, Swan Hunter (builders of such liners as the legendary *Mauretania* of 1907) closed down last year and, symptomatic, most of the towering cranes sold and carted off to India.

Travel to Alnwick, about 30 miles away, to see the local castle, owned and still occupied by the Duke and Duchess of Northumberland. But really off on my own for a bit: into the village to see the White Swan Hotel, which has a dining room and lounge with fine wood paneling from the liner *Olympic*, sister ship to the *Titanic* and herself scrapped locally at Jarrow in 1936. Along with the scrap metal, the wood was sold off to raise money in those hard-pressed Depression-era times. Pristine and polished and balanced by fine stained-glass windows flooded by great autumn afternoon sunlight, the hotel space is splendid and indeed well worth the visit. The castle, the setting for parts of the *Harry Potter* films, is fairytale-like: towers, gates, great velvety green lawns. The duke's apartments are expectedly stunning: a vast library, magnificent carpets, glistening chandeliers, a private chapel and a grand dining room seating 24. And the countryside to and from Alnwick is expectedly picture perfect: corn-colored rolling fields, emerald-colored hillsides, quaint villages dotted by miniature stone churches. The October light, especially through the trees, casts the wonderful glows, giving the most gorgeously sentimental effects.

Thursday, 9 October

Last full day of this hugely sentimental voyage. Art auction this morning … Robert Lloyd's magnificent view of the *QE2* anchored in the Mersey at Liverpool is auctioned to great success. The top bidder is none other than Commodore Warwick. His winning bid: $14,000. The oversized ship's charts for this voyage fetch $6,000 and other charts between $2-4,000. The monies go to the Prince's Trust, which Cunard itself helps sponsor. My 11:00am lecture about the Cunard *Queens* brings forth several company crewmembers from the 1950s and two shipyard workers from the building of the *QE2* in 1966-67 and, of course, some former passengers

from the original *Mary* and *Elizabeth* in the '50s. I sign books at 3:30 and, happily, we see over 300 Bill Miller books going home as souvenirs. By afternoon, the mood is increasingly somber – the knowledge by many that this is their very last night aboard this iconic, much-beloved ship. 'There will never, ever be another *QE2*,' says a lady from Inverness with slight tears in her eyes. Another lady from London adds, 'I am booked next year for the *QM2* and the *Queen Victoria* as well, but neither ship is quite the same as the *QE2*. I shall miss her very much.'

Ever charming and always so kind, Captain McNaught signs various items for me – the golden keepsakes of a cherished ship on a most memorable voyage.

Friday, 10 October

Disembarkation: crowds, suitcases, those last exchanges of contact information. Gone in the first wave by 7:00am, Michael is off – and in a flash change of plans and heading to Berlin and Prague for a four-night stay and then homeward to New Jersey on Wed. More leisurely and quite local, I go off to Mayflower Park here in Southampton for a close-up of the *Queen Mary 2*, which has just arrived from New York. The *QE2* is berthed a mile away at the Queen Elizabeth II Terminal.

Des (Kirkpatrick) arrives at noon and becomes my cabin mate for the six-day westward crossing to Manhattan, arriving next Thursday morning, the 16th. The *QE2* is fully booked for her final run to America, after 806 trips and 710 visits to New York since her maiden call there in May 1969. Altogether, the 70,000-ton ship has the greatest records of any big ocean liner in history: 1,428 voyages in 39 years, clocking 5.9 million miles, carrying 2½ million passengers and making 25 90- to 100-day world cruises. Lots of familiar faces aboard: Ted Scull (the well-known ocean liner writer and lecturer), Gary Buchanan (one of Britain's top cruise journalists), Brian Hoey (who lectures about the royals), David Hume (chairman of the World Ship Society in Manhattan), countless ship buffs and a small army of Cunard and maritime commemorative enthusiasts. 'I've done 30 cruises, but never one on the *QE2*,' said a Florida retiree. 'I felt I must do the *Queen* at least once and on one of her historic final voyages. I booked 15 months ago and have looked forward ever since.'

Under gorgeous autumn, sun-filled skies, the grand procession begins at 5:00pm – the mighty *Ventura*, 118,000 tons and the largest P&O liner to date, sails first and, through her whistles, salutes the waiting, but soon-to-depart *Elizabeth 2*; the gleaming, towering *QM2* follows and, in something of royal protocol, waits to take up the rear as the *QE2* goes next and fills center position. The decks of the *Elizabeth* are crammed with plastic-flag-waving well-wishers and sentimentalists. Run into all sorts of people – including Stephen Berry, whom I visited in his ship-memorabilia-filled high-rise apartment overlooking Sydney harbor and its famed arch bridge in 1984 and again in '86, but have not seen since. Also meet up with many others including Martin and Ahmet, friends from London, but not seen for four years. Cheerful reunions!

Saturday, 11 October
My first lecture to, quite thankfully, a huge audience – not a seat and the overflow reaching out into the corridors beyond the two doors in that Upper Deck theater. Thomas Quinones, the Cruise Host, gives the most rousing introduction … pure operatic! Afterward, at a book signing, the high spirits continue – we sell and I sign 150 books in an hour! One lady from Edinburgh buys ten books – one for each of her grandchildren. The chats, while quick and slightly controlled, produce retired sea captains, ocean liner model builders and scores of passengers from many bygone liners, especially Cunard. 'I was a young GI onboard the *Queen Mary* in 1944,' says one now elderly man supported by two canes. Another man, silver-haired and beautifully spoken, tells me he was a captain on the old British India Line and hints of his adventures visiting ports in India and the Middle East.

After dinner, my good friend and superb entertainer Petrina Johnson gives a rousing show in the Main Lounge. Including wonderful imitations of the likes of Garland, Streisand and Dolly Parton, we are in front-row seats to cheer the dear lady on. On the high seas these days, she is one of the very best!

Sunday, 12 October
Brian's lecture on Buckingham Palace and then Ted's talk on the life and times of the *QE2* fill out the day – which includes white-gloved tea at 4 in the grand Queens Room. By 3:15, there's not a seat to be had. Outside, through the big windows, the *QM2* is on the port side, pitching and her bulbous bow poking upwards at times, all while shining in bouts of bright sunlight. She looks quite magnificent, certainly a symbol of nautical power and might and, I suspect, will replace the *QE2* in the hearts and minds of the traveling public. While the *QE2* has a very definite 'soul', a very rare ocean liner quality, the *Mary 2* has developed one as well in her five years of service.

Chat with Captain McNaught and he tells us that the latest rumor from Dubai, the ship's new home, is that the symbolic funnel will come off

in the conversion and become a multi-level luxury apartment, the finest quarters to be onboard. Later, someone else tells us that he hears that the funnel will become the main entrance to the ship's innards through glass-enclosed, tubular extensions from shore, from Palm Island. A third rumor floating about is that the *QE2* will cut in half and lengthened and that all the lifeboats along the Boat Deck will be removed and then converted to apartments.

Monday, 13 October
More lectures fill the day: Ted doing liners around the world and much about his own travels in them, Brian on the life and times of the royal yacht *Britannia* and Major Michael Parker on organizing the Queen's jubilee celebrations. Ted, Doug Ward and I host a ship-buff chat group in the Crystal Bar at 4. All sorts of questions and comments and of course rather heavy regrets that the *QE2* is ending her sailing days and finishing up in Dubai.

Otherwise, morning chat with big contingent of French ship buffs (including author of a superb book on the great *France*) and then lunch with Stephen Berry, who I have not seen in some 25 years. Yes, ships in the night since then.

Youngish, very bright businessman, in his 40s, tells me after tea that he has lost an amount totaling in seven figures in the current financial crash and whirlwind. Like others, including a bank vice-president from Boston, the prognosis is not good – perhaps five years or longer before any signs of recovery!

Gleaming like some big, jewel-encrusted brooch, the *QM2* is just outside our window, less than a mile away, and glowing on that coal-colored horizon.

Tuesday, 14 October
Off Newfoundland, now two days from New York harbor and calming seas and clearer skies. The last of my lectures and then at 3:30pm we have a special showing of 'Lady in Waiting: The Story of the SS *United States*'. Unseen by the Brits and other Europeans and even a good number of the Yankee guests, everyone is full of compliments, praises, but also sad and sentimental feelings for that once-great, but now almost derelict liner. Any chances of her being even remotely revived were sealed shut and closed after the recent weeks of financial downturns. One older gent adds a note, 'You looked much younger in that film.' Of course, it was filmed just a year ago. Oh, well … it must have been the lighting.

Sold another 75 or so books today … indeed, record sales for the *QE2* or any Cunarder … but signing pens and those big flourishes and of course 'Farewell *QE2*' notations and inscriptions. Between these two trips, the librarians guess that we have sold 400-500 of my books in total. The British and some German guests are noted big buyers.

Tea in the Queens Grill with Martin and Ahmet, friends from prior voyages who kindly invite me to London and to stay at their apartment in Pimlico. Later, drinks in Captain McNaught's quarters … a very kind invitation, but which is overcrowded … 60 or so guests, all in formal wear, squeeze in the small office, sip champagne and chat on often with great big smiles and nodding heads. A Cunard officer observes, 'Life aboard the liners means developing skill at aimless chatter. You are most tested usually at dinner tables and at cocktail parties like these. It is often the same questions and, to these beautifully dressed people who have spent lots of money just to come, you just smile and nod and simplify the responses – and often for the 1,000th time.' A lady spills her champagne, another old dear feels faint. A Manhattan banker notes, 'Onboard ships like the *QE2*, we are, if only temporarily, cut off from the real world. And so, as we sip drinks here, munch snacks and chat away, we barely have to think beyond tomorrow's breakfast.'

Masquerade ball in the elegant Queens Room and chat with Dr Doris, known also as Dancing Doris, who spends nine months a year on cruise ships, usually Cunard and Crystal. A brilliant woman who invented some special formula for Union Carbide, she took to cruising after retirement, but almost completely to play bridge. But when that game was canceled one day, the bored Doris opted to take a dance class. She was then 84. Now, at 96, she dances every night of the voyage, from 8 onwards to well after 12. And like racehorses, she rates the dance hosts and follows some to other ships. She is, of course, having the greatest fun.

Wednesday, 15 October

Final day … packing starting in the afternoon … discussion group in the main lounge at 11 on the SS *France/Norway* and of course well attended by ship buffs.

We arrive tomorrow at Pier 88, at West 48th Street, landing at 6:00am. It is of course the last visit of the great *Queen Elizabeth 2* and her final time to sail up along the Hudson. The *QM2* arrives as well, but goes to Red Hook in Brooklyn, and then the two great Cunarders depart, again in tandem, but eastbound back to Southampton, at 5:00pm. I am to film (at 7:30am) for a documentary about the *QE2*, all organized by Cunard

Public Relations and a sentimental testament and reflection about this iconic ship. But then ashore and my own goodbyes! Overall, it is all quite good – mega-rich Dubai will be a great home and caretaker to the celebrated, world-famous ship. Three blasts and good luck to the *QE2*!

Thursday, 16 October

6:00am arrival into New York harbor … that grand skyline veiled in moody mists, even foggy patches … the lights of the Lower Manhattan towers seem almost vaporous … even the glorious Woolworth, normally poised and glowing, is but a shadowy silhouette. The stately *QE2* makes her final trek along the mighty Hudson, her last time along those famed West Side piers. A long, busy, people-filled day. By 7:30, together with Cunard's publicity team (Brian, Jackie, Michael and others), I join the 'forces' and film for the evening news. Segments are 'fanned' out throughout the country and perhaps a little beyond and so, with reserved but still smiling faces, we talk of the great *Queen*, her life and times, her records, her love affair with the public and – the big hook – her next life out in the Middle East.

We film on the upper decks with that big orange-red smokestack as the perfect background prop and then, across the slip at West 51st Street, from the rooftop of Pier 92 and using great chunks of the *QE2*'s midsection (berthed at Pier 90) as the backup set. The full cast is out: Captain McNaught, Commodore Warner (brought over by car from the *Queen Mary 2*, which is docked over in Red Hook, Brooklyn) and, of course, Carol Marlow. Then back aboard: 150 or so guests for drinks onboard, in the Yacht Club Lounge, and then to lunch in the Caronia Restaurant. I sit at Commodore Warner's table, joining the British Ambassador to the USA and a few heavy players from the New York travel world. 'Yes, we are worried about the future in these changing economic times,' commented the impeccably uniformed commodore. 'We worry if we will have enough passengers to fill our beautiful ships, especially in the months ahead.' The lunch is set, the menus specially printed and everyone gets a goodbye present. By 3, with a slight turn of my head, it is off and then across the gangway for the very last time. Indeed, a favorite ship in so many ways and 39 years and 35 trips in her of memories and reflections and events.

The elements played their part to absolute perfection. It was the great exit scene, the stirring piece in the glorious maritime operetta. Late on an autumn afternoon, battleship gray clouds were looming as otherwise rather milky sunlight cast a soft glow on the skyline of Manhattan. Other thickening clouds soon formed, the winds kicked up a bit and then there was mist and some drops of October rain. Soon, above the harbor were *Wizard of Oz* skies! Aboard a specially chartered harbor ferry, several hundred of us had eyes and cameras mostly fixed, however, on the north berth of Pier 90. The iconic *Queen Elizabeth 2* was in her final hour in port, soon to be undocked by two Moran tugs and then sent on her way. It was, of course, hardly an ordinary departure.

The 70,000-ton Cunarder was leaving New York, after 710 visits, for the last time. Unquestionably the most beloved, famous and possibly popular passenger ship afloat, sentiments ran deep and often high – saddened smiles, great hand waves of goodbye, some tears of course. Many onlookers had happy memories of the 963ft-long ship, from aboard her countless voyages. (Altogether, the 32-knot ship has the greatest records of any big ocean liner in history: 1,428 voyages, clocking 5.9 million miles, carrying 2½ million passengers and making 25 90-100 day world cruises.) Finally, the throaty whistles sounded, the *Queen* was undocked and then sent southward along the Hudson, where she joined her successor of sorts, the far bigger and taller *Queen Mary 2*, which had departed from Cunard's Brooklyn terminal and which was waiting off the Battery. Then, with roaring whistle exchanges, the two great liners departed together – the *QE2* in the lead, of course, and as both ships glowed much like diamonds against the deep purple skies of twilight. New York harbor was at its most romantic, the two ships stunning and almost ethereal, the mood exciting, almost exhilarating and yet poetically sentimental, even quite sad.

Home by 9:00pm … quite exhausted … hand-shaked and smiled and chatted out … and with good doses of emotion … and enthusiasm … and chatter … and that cool, autumny, Hudson river air. Seeing Manhattan aglow – indeed, those glistening, glowing diamonds – those gorgeous towers, reaching for the sky, vying with one another for attention, individual and unique and positively solid – and from the decks of that charter boat was in itself magic. It was the Hollywood set, pure Cole Porter, unquestionably the Fred & Ginger set piece.

FAREWELL BELOVED LADY

Etta and Ann Uttley are longtime loyalists to the QE2. Among their many voyages, the mother and daughter were aboard the iconic liner's Farewell to the British Isles cruise in October 2008 and then the Farewell Voyage to Dubai. Ann penned a reflection of that final voyage.

The *Queen* was waiting for us – but this time she was waiting for the last time. I always knew this day would have to come – but not now, not today. We watched the million poppies being dropped by the planes on her at 11am for Remembrance Day from Westin shore with our friends. The poppies blew over to us. It was so moving that she should leave her home on this the eleventh day of the eleventh month, so poignant. We picked up some of the fallen poppies as keepsakes. Emotions were so mixed. In ways, it felt just like a normal *QE2* cruise – the build-up of excitement to the great day, the travelling to Southampton, and arrival at the Queen Elizabeth II Terminal and the first glimpse of that mighty red and black funnel. The sight of that funnel always gives me goose bumps. But even if it felt like it did before, I realized I really have to drink this all in and remember every minute as this moment will never ever happen again and not just for me but for everyone. We made our way to the gangway for boarding. We were almost there. It was like home. The *QE2* feels so familiar to us, so welcoming, so beautiful. Simply, you enter another world when you step on board. It's wonderful. No other ship can give us this feeling. She casts her magic spell from the moment you step onto those famous decks.

After our white-gloved escort to our stateroom, we are pleased to see our luggage is waiting for us, having been stored in the baggage room on board from our previous voyage. That's something that will never be heard of again. No ship – whether called a liner or not – has this privilege today, sadly this is probably because of security, but it is so civilized to arrive in your stateroom and find your luggage waiting for you. We also have our complimentary bottles of champagne, gifts from Cunard, and we share this as we absorb the moment again and never to be repeated. Happily, we find we are seated at the captain's table for this entire special final voyage. Of course, we are delighted! What a privilege! We just love the glamour of it all.

The departure from Southampton in the dark was not as emotional as I thought it would be, however. We couldn't see the thousands of people who had turned out on this cold November night to see us off. Had it been a daylight sailing, it would have been so different as the spectators wanted to have their photos of the ship sailing out and see all the hundreds of small craft follow us out. The deep darkness just gives a really haunting perspective. We could easily have sailed the next morning after having the fireworks, etc., the previous evening. The people of Southampton wanted that too, but Cunard ruled the roost.

Standing on the aft deck watching the wake of this wonderful ship is always an unforgettable experience. We are now on the Bay of Biscay. To 'feel' that power beneath you as QE2 effortlessly cuts through the water is simply amazing. She slices through the waves, seemingly hardly disturbing the ocean, yet at her high speed appears to just kiss the top of the waves as she sails on serenely. Even at 41 years of age, she can outrun the rest. Truly, I feel it is such a waste to retire her, but that of course is merely the opinion of a very devoted passenger. I don't see what's under the bonnet, nor the mileage on the clock. Emotionally, we just want to keep her forever.

But this final voyage of the most famous ship in the world was a little disappointing as we felt that no real effort was put in by Cunard themselves to make it special for their passengers. Only the departure at Southampton and then the arrival at Dubai were the highlights (and none of which were funded by Cunard themselves). We did feel we were only there to accompany the ship to her final resting place and, of course, paid an excessively high premium for the privilege. Whilst we were delighted to actually be there, of course, and be part of history, we did think more could have been put on for us. Many other passengers felt the same way. We had thought we would have some big names to entertain us, for example, and for which Cunard still pride themselves on in their advertising. Actually, this only happened at the last minute on the last night at Dubai when Des O'Connor came aboard to entertain us as well as the Beatles Tribute Band, who left the ship in Malta, but were flown out again from the UK to Dubai to join the ship. This was all very strange indeed. Obviously, a last-minute decision was made, as many passengers had been complaining about the lack of quality entertainment on such a high-profile ship. Des O'Connor did not stay on board. It felt like a normal QE2 cruise.

Our arrivals and departures at the ports on the way attracted very little or no attention whatsoever. The exception was Malta, who provided a gun salute on our arrival and a few small crowds on our departure. At our final port of Alexandria, we spent some time walking on and off the ship continuously. We must be crazy you might think. But then only truly devoted QE2 fans would realise that this would be the absolute last time to walk up that famous gangway to board QE2 and sail to the next port. Yes, it was the very last time. This was when I shed my first tears. It was the full realisation that this ship was retiring and that was finally starting to sink in. Upon leaving Alexandria, our

final port of call after 40 years of sailing the world's oceans, we had no sail-away celebrations whatsoever. It was unbelievable. A small group of about a half-dozen passengers standing next to us began to sing 'Auld Lang Syne' as we pulled away. Sadly, there was nobody on the quayside to wave our last farewell. It was quite heartbreaking.

We had to sail into Dubai a day early so as to arrive in daylight at the request of the new owners. Some passengers had mixed feelings over this, as it did in fact take the last night at sea away from us and therefore changing a lot of passengers' plans to enjoy the very last night at sea. The arrival at Dubai was very memorable, with the Sultan's yacht leading us in and a Royal Naval Escort, which for the first time in history gave a full naval salute to a ship of the merchant marine. This was very special indeed. All the sailors were out on deck in their whites and cheered three times, lifting their hats to the QE2. It was terribly emotional, especially as everyone on the decks cheered and cheered – until we were quite hoarse. After all, she was still British, still ours, well for another few hours at least. We felt so proud. An Emirates Airbus A380 did several flypasts over the ship and gave all the passengers the opportunity for good photos to take home and show their friends and families. Later, after docking at Port Rashid, everything just seemed normal, quite like any other arrival.

There was no announcement of 'finished with engines' or anything. We expected something special. We had a firework display at 6pm, but which was shortened due to the fact that Dubai Airport had to be closed as the display was right on the flight path. The decks were crowded to witness this final celebration. I stood under the bridge wing on the port side and happened to look up at the bridge to see Captain McNaught and various VIPs out to watch the display. This included the executives of Nakheel (the new owners) standing there resplendently in their national dress. This was the exact moment that I now knew that QE2 had gone. It hit me hard, the tears ran down my cheeks. She wasn't ours anymore. But I know many could be thankful that Dubai will give her a new chapter in her life instead of going for scrap. But like many others on deck that night, our families built her, with their sweat and toil in Scotland, and now these 'strangers' are taking her away from us. In many ways, I was glad that my uncles were not here to witness this day. Why? I cannot explain it, but they came from another generation. The pride of building this magnificent vessel, the hard times, the heritage! We feel she 'belongs' to us. She is ours. She will not belong to some far-off land, where customs and cultures are miles apart.

This last night on board the most famous and beautiful ship in the world will be remembered for a very long time. The dress code is informal, but like many other passengers, we decide we will go formal – indeed, as a tribute to this grand Queen of the Seas! After all, she always put on her Sunday best for us every time. So we all go for it! She has to go out with a bang! I wear my most spectacular evening gown in black taffeta with a train and specially embroidered with the ship herself (and which proves a real talking point on board). As a tribute to this wonderful ship, I decided I must have this dress on the date it was announced she was to be retired, on 18 June 2008. Fortunately, I am a dressmaker and this project was put into full swing with amazing results. It was my very own way of saying 'thank you' to her for all the wonderful years and wonderful memories on board.

After the final dinner in the Caronia Restaurant, we had a wonderful show in the Grand Lounge with Des O'Connor entertaining. Afterwards, we made our way to the Queens Room for the very last QE2 performance of her career as an ocean-going liner. The program was highlighted with the magnificent voice of Annette Wardell and the fabulous QE2 orchestra. Later, we all took to the floor and joined hands to sing 'Auld Lang Syne'. It was highly emotional. We couldn't see through the tears. It was happening now. This was it – the last night, the last time. It was quite unbearable.

Finally, in a more upbeat mood, the Beatles Tribute Band put on an unexpected performance up in the grand lounge and passengers joined crew on the dance floor and danced the night away throwing balloons and laughing and hugging each other goodbye. This continued till about 2am. Later, we had a last turn around those famous teak decks, touching the rails. Looking up at that wonderful illuminated red funnel with smoke still drifting across the starlit Arabian sky, I looked over to the swimming pool – the loungers are all piled high as if ready for the next sunny day on deck. Everything looked as it should be for another day on the high seas. She was permanently stationary now; this was her new home and this is where she will remain for her lifetime. It was hard to take it all in. We said our goodnight to her and made our way back to our stateroom. We had experienced QE2 for the very last time. The ship was dying – and a little piece of us was dying with her ...

That night I truly cried. I realised it was the end. I couldn't stop, feeling quite daft really. But I just couldn't help it – and there were many other passengers feeling the same way. The packing was done for the very last time, no doubt many passengers had their cases bulging with a lot of 'extra' souvenirs taken from the ship. We were advised we could take many items with us and with Cunard's authority, but actually many things seemed to disappear throughout the voyage! What did I take you may ask? Perhaps a few signs from the deck or a cup and saucer? No, nothing like that. I did take the Bible from my stateroom. That was rather odd perhaps. There is no significance where it came from, no Cunard or QE2 imprinted. But I know where it came from (and there was no point in leaving it in a Muslim country. I am not particularly religious, but have hope and faith that QE2 will live on for many years to come in a different guise. So, it is a special little part of QE2 that I can hold onto and remember such an iconic ship, the one that touched the hearts not just of a nation, but the entire world.

On the last morning, it's an early final breakfast in the dining room. This was truly the final goodbye. The emotions were running high, both with passengers and crew alike. There was a subdued atmosphere never felt before. There was a hushed, eerie silence. The ship was actually being emptied as we sat eating our breakfast. I could not bear it.

We walked off the gangway with such heavy hearts. We do hope she will remain for many years to come, but know she will look very different and not be the QE2 we have known and worshipped for many years. This was it. We will not return to see her again.

As the coach made its way out of the port, I filmed the final moments on my camcorder. I never thought it would hurt as much, I was blinded by tears and could barely speak. I looked back till she faded into the distance. Farewell QE2!

Later, I asked myself how just a ship can make me feel this way. Was it is because of all the wonderful happy memories of sailing onboard all those years? Was it because she has been so special to us or because she was so stunningly beautiful? Then I think further for a moment and then I realise, quite simply: it is because she is so truly loved.

Ann Uttley also penned a poem marking the farewell of her favorite Cunarder:

Opposite page:
Above: The moody autumn afternoon light made for a dramatic setting for the farewell departure from New York. (Robert O'Brien Collection).

Middle: The lighted funnel stands out against the various, ever-changing colors of that October afternoon. (Robert O'Brien Collection).

Below: With the *Queen Mary 2* having departed from Brooklyn in the Upper Bay, the two *Queens* meet off Jersey City. (Robert O'Brien Collection).

QE2: If I Could Have My Say ...

Life begins at forty so I have been told
But it seems my Cunard owners now think that I'm too old
I thought I'd get a makeover, a little nip'n'tuck
As you see I didn't get it, no such bloomin' luck

I was born in Scotland on the Bonnie banks o' Clyde
When I went down that slipway, how my heart filled up with pride
I only had one funnel; I looked a wee bit odd
But then you must remember, I was a swingin' '60s mod!
My cruising days are over; no more Atlantic run
No more cocktail parties, O the laughter and the fun
I've sailed around the world, now 6 million miles or so
But now at 41 years old, I'm told I have to go

I loved the North Atlantic when I was sailing fast
No other ship could beat me; they were always last
I've got to take retirement; I'm sailing to the sun
Nobody thought to tell me my sailing days were done

My home was in Southampton, a berth down by the Solent
Where my every departure was a very special moment
Now it's time to say goodbye; you can't know how I feel
I've to go to endless sunshine where my skin will burn and peel

I sailed into Dubai today, the Sultan's yacht was here
But now they've left me all alone and my heart is filled with fear
My engines now lie silent, the command from Captain Mac
But I know that he wanted to turn round and take me back

I've now got brand new owners; I think they're called Nakheel
But they don't speak my language, so they don't know how I feel
If they would only ask me what I'm thinking, if I could only have my say
It would be to sail out on the Ocean just for one more day

They say I'm going to dry dock for a year or two
Are they going to hurt me o what are they going to do?
Have you seen the papers ... there's been a bit of trouble
I heard a rumor yesterday, they are cutting off my funnel!

Now I am so far away on this foreign eastern shore
I want to go back home now but they don't want me any more
I want to live FOREVER, to sail the ocean blue
So we can be together, such is my love for you

So will you come and see me on this Palm where I can dream
And will YOU always remember that I was once a Queen?
Southampton gets my anchor; they all want to have a part
But what's for Bonnie Scotland ... to my home I left my heart

Above left: Miss Liberty seems to stand on the foredeck as the *QE2* takes the lead. (Robert O'Brien Collection).

Above right: With whistles sounding, passengers cheering and cameras flashing, the two *Queens* made for a most extraordinary sight as they departed simultaneously on that moodful October evening. (Cunard Line).

Left: The *QE2* and the *Queen Mary 2* create a most fascinating comparison in ocean liner design of some 40 years. (Robert O'Brien Collection).

Monday, 11 November

Richard Faber, the noted, New York City-based ocean liner collector and seller, began sailing onboard the *QE2* in 1975. Expectedly, he quickly booked the ship's final sailing for Cunard. 'Back in the '70s, the *Queen* became the "only way to cross". I loved every voyage aboard her and always looked forward to the next,' he recounted. 'In 1999, during the ship's 30th-anniversary cruise with a large contingent of ship enthusiasts and historians onboard, I met Captain Ron Warwick and a great friendship developed. This was a great step forward in my love affair with the *Queen*. I was now addicted to the ship. I began sailing on her two or three times a year. The *QE2* did not move to second place in my heart and affection until the *QM2* arrived and with now Commodore Warwick aboard and in command. But when the *QE2*'s retirement was announced, I felt it was very special. It was 33 years of association, of memories, of having a special ship in my life. The Dubai voyage was something quite extraordinary. I knew it would be very special and so, a year and half in advance, in June 2007, I booked a Princess Grill cabin.

Richard Faber arrived in Southampton the night before the final departure. 'There were some tense moments the next morning, on the 11th,' he remembered. 'We heard on the 6:30am morning news on the hotel television that the *QE2* was inbound, but aground on a sandbank. But happily, she was quickly refloated and later boarded at 12 noon. To mark the occasion, Prince Philip was aboard for lunch. We later saw him and other top Cunard officials and guests on the outer aft deck as a Harrier jet hovered over the ship in salute. That night, there was a big, gala departure. It was very dark. But there were breathtaking fireworks and the sounds of whistles and horns seemed to go on forever.'

Tuesday, 12 November

'As the last Cunard passengers, we began getting settled on this first day,' recalled Richard Faber. 'We were all eager for special entertainment, but there were no specific lectures, especially ones about the ship and Cunard's great history. Later, the port calls were uneventful. There were no flotillas of tugs or spraying fireboats or grand send-offs. At Naples, as an example, the lights in the terminal were switched off before we actually left the pier.

'Malta had fireworks, however, and lots of whistle blowing,' he added. 'Later, at Alexandria, we made our first visit to Egypt. It was all very memorable, exciting and included a visit to the pyramids. In the Suez Canal, there was no wait and so no delays. Three days later, we arrived in Dubai. The voyage was coming to a close.'

Expert ocean liner collector Albert Wilhelmi was also aboard the farewell sailing to Dubai. 'I had my first trip on the *QE2* in 1979 and this Farewell Voyage was our sixth voyage aboard her. I was absolutely delighted to find her in the very best condition ever. The ship was just immaculate, just sparkling and gleaming and polished from end to end,' he said. Food and service in the Caronia Restaurant also surpassed that of any previous voyage on the *Queen* and, in fact, even surpassed that onboard the *Queen Mary 2*. In addition, the *QE2* has remained very elegant. She was one of the last ships with a full dress code. It was all very elegant and included the likes of three formal nights in succession.'

Wednesday, 26 November

'The arrival in Dubai was an all-afternoon affair,' remembered Richard Faber. 'There were lots of harbor craft to greet us as well as a British destroyer and a Dubai royal yacht. An Airbus 380 hovered overhead. We arrived at Port Rashid at 5:30pm, just as darkness fell. It was now our final night onboard.

'The last night was the usual Cunard operation, but at pierside. It was all very ordinary except for a gala farewell at midnight in the Queens Room, which included dancing and then a sing-along.'

Thursday, 27 November

'Almost as if on any ordinary voyage, we disembarked immediately after breakfast,' added Faber. 'We seemed too unfazed, possibly masking our feelings or avoiding them. The Nakheel Corporation formally took possession of the ship later that day. The Cunard era for the *QE2* was over.'

Friday, 28 November

'From a taxi, we had our last close-up look at the *QE2* at the pier. The crew were disembarking and it was a very sad moment to witness,' concluded Faber. 'The ship was now flying the Dubai flag. We then headed to the airport and the conclusion of this very special trip. We wanted the trip to be deluxe from start to finish. We flew home [to New York City] on Emirates Airlines and in first class, which was reputed to be amongst the very finest in air travel. We did not have a seat, but a suite. First class was a private compartment. It was 14 hours to New York of complete pampering and unlimited champagne, caviar and fine food.

'Once at home, I felt the full loss of the *QE2*. It hit me! I began to feel very sad. But I also felt relieved, even excited, about having the *QM2*. She is my new favorite liner. These days, Cunard has a product that is consistently first rate in every way. I know exactly what I am getting. For me, there is absolutely no reason to go on another line. When I sail with Cunard, there are no disappointments. Yes, there are still links to history, but it is more about shipboard tradition. It is all about understated British-style service. Simply, there are no gimmicks. It is just wholesome, good service.'

Regarding a voyage that included his first-ever transit of the Suez Canal, Albert Wilhelmi continued his high praises for the grand Cunarder. 'Throughout the voyage from Southampton to Dubai, she rode beautifully. The crew was excellent and the ever-friendly Captain McNaught is pure charm. He spoke to everyone, it seemed.

'We had perfect weather and it became warmer each day. Gibraltar was special. I loved Naples and enjoyed Malta and Egypt and, of course, the passage through the Suez Canal. That portion of the trip was quite historic and romantic, and reminded me of the great days of the P&O liners going out east. But our arrival in Dubai was absolutely fantastic. The prince's mega-yacht came out to meet us and there was a flyover by one of the big, double-decked Emirates Airlines' jets.'

After countless voyages on numerous ships beginning in the 1960s, Wilhelmi remained thrilled with the chance to sail the legendary QE2 one more time. 'It was one of the very best voyages we ever made. Throughout the cruise, the ship had a certain aura. And our fellow passengers were delightful, if sentimental sometimes. The end of the QE2 as a Cunard liner really did not hit you until the end. For me, even the last day didn't quite sink in. Others were very emotional. The fact that the QE2 would not sail again really hit me later, once I was back at home. I felt a great loss.'

Another world-class ocean liner collector, Mario Pulice made fourteen trips onboard the QE2. Clearly, the Cunarder is one of his favorite ships. 'I had been aboard the 40th Anniversary Voyage Around Britain in 2007,' he reported. 'On the very last night of that voyage, there were endless toasts and loud applause. There was this great, very visible emotion, a deep sentimentality. But, quite surprisingly, on the last night on that last voyage to Dubai, it was all very ordinary. I was seated in the Princess Grill

and there were no toasts and, in the end, everyone just seemed to say "good night". The passengers were, I think, in denial. They did not want to acknowledge that it was the end. In itself, that was the great sadness within the sad ending that was the ship's final Cunard voyage. There were lots more tears and visible emotions on that 40th-anniversary cruise. There had been these eloquent speeches about what the QE2 meant to the British people and how she was a part of Britain itself. You could feel the heartfelt emotions. People had been deeply moved by this mass of steel.

'The general condition of the 39-year-old ship was excellent,' added Pulice. 'Before sailing, I thought that she might be threadbare, rundown, dowdy. But it seems she had to be delivered in top condition. The quality of the food and level of service was also as good as ever. It was very sentimental on the last few days to see packing boxes lining the corridors. We realized that the end was near. The onboard shops had endless sales before Dubai. In the end, it was 75-80 per cent off just about every item. By the last day, the shops were empty. The synagogue had been closed and some artwork was coming down. The staff was very understated. Everyone was, or so it seemed, very stoic. One senior officer simply said, "It's time – time to go!"'

Mario Pulice recalled the very last morning after the ship's arrival in Dubai. 'I had walked around the seemingly empty ship the night before. The decks were desolate. It seemed that everyone had gone to bed early. Myself, during my walk, I "thanked" the ship for all the great times, the wonderful memories. I thought: "See you again sometime!" I touched the wood, felt the furniture, inhaled the smell of the ship. Actually, it all felt quite bizarre. Even I was in denial. On the following morning, I just walked off. I felt that the QE2 now exists somewhere else. The sense of loss did not really hit me until I returned to New York. I felt confident and hopeful, however. I just hope that her Dubai owners have the proper respect and the feel for her great history. For myself, I was hopeful even. I thought I might even see the ship again! The ship has changed so often and often quite drastically over the years. So, this is her next change out in far-away Dubai. She is indestructible – she just goes on!'

Above left: Gala fireworks signaled the *QE2's* final departure from Southampton. (Richard Faber Collection).

Above right: On her Farewell Cruise, sailing to Dubai, the *QE2* called at Gibraltar, where she is seen here with the Spanish cruise ship *Zenith*. (Richard Faber Collection).

Right: Happy travelers fill the stern decks of the *QE2* on her final Cunard cruise. (Richard Faber Collection).

Clockwise, from top left: A full salute to maritime royalty at Valletta on Malta, November 18th 2008. (Richard Faber Collection).

The final transit of the Suez Canal.

Above: The *QE2*'s funnel in the evening sun, Dubai.

Above right: Creative pastries on the final cruise. (Richard Faber Collection)

Right: Passenger Stanley Haviland used one of his favorite ships, berthed at Valletta, as an otherwise joyous Christmas card. (Stanley Haviland Collection).

Dubai's royal yacht, the largest and most luxurious of its kind in the world, leads the *QE2* into Port Rashid. (Richard Faber Collection).

Above: A brand-new Emirates Airlines 777 salutes the inbound *QE2*. (Richard Faber Collection.

Below: Passenger luggage at the final Cunard disembarkation. (Richard Faber Collection).

Above: Captain Ian McNaught watches over the transition – from arrival, final disembarkation and then the handover and follow-up from Cunard to the new Dubai owners. (Richard Faber Collection).

Below: The *QE2* is in her new home waters. (Richard Faber Collection).

With the British flag lowered, the colors of Dubai now fly from the stern of the *QE2*. (Richard Faber Collection).

Left: Indeed, a nighttime addition to the skyline at Port Rashid. (Richard Faber Collection).

Below left: Slowly, the QE2 became visible through the haze.

Below right: The final arrival and disembarkation. The ship's Cunard days were coming to a close. (Richard Faber Collection).

Right: A final glimpse – the iconic, much-beloved
Queen Elizabeth 2. (Richard Faber Collection)

Overleaf: The handover!.

BIBLIOGRAPHY

Devol, George & Thomas Cassidy (eds.), *Ocean & Cruise News* (Northport, New York: World Ocean & Cruise Society, 1980-2009)

Mayes, William, *Cruise Ships* (Windsor, England: Overview Press Ltd, 2005)
Miller, William H., *The QE2: A Picture History* (Mineola, New York: Dover Publications Inc., 2008)

Warwick, Ronald, *QE2* (New York: W. W. Norton & Company Inc., 1993)